AN ILLUSTRATED GUIDE TO
MODERN
WARSHIPS

AN ILLUSTRATED GUIDE TO
MODERN
WARSHIPS

Hugh Lyon

a Salamander book

Published by Arco Publishing, Inc.
NEW YORK

A Salamander Book

Published by
Arco Publishing, Inc.,
219 Park Avenue South,
New York,
N.Y. 10003,
United States of America.

© 1980 by Salamander Books Ltd.,
27 Old Gloucester Street,
London WC1N 3AF,
United Kingdom.

ISBN 0-668-04966-9

Contents

Ships are arranged alphabetically within national groups.

Credits

Author: Hugh Lyon, former Research Officer of the Shipbuilding Record Survey, London, founder-member of the Warships Society, and contributor to many technical defence periodicals and books.

(The publishers wish to thank David Miller for his assistance in the preparation of this book)

Editor: Ray Bonds
Designer: Lloyd Martin

Line drawings: © Siegfried Breyer and © A.D. Baker (US warships, courtesy *Jane's Fighting Ships*)
Photographs: The publishers wish to thank all the official international governmental archives, weapons systems manufacturers and private collections who supplied photographs for this book.

Printed in Belgium by Henri Proost et Cie.

DD 280 Class

Destroyers

Four ships: *Iroquois* (DD 280), *Huron* (DD 281), *Athabaskan* (DD282), *Algonquin* (DD 283).

Country of origin: Canada
Displacement: 4700 tons full load.
Dimensions: Length overall 426ft (129·8m); beam 50ft (15·2m); draught 14·5ft (4·4m).
Aircraft: Two Sikorsky Sea King helicopters (CH-SS-2).
Armament: Two quadruple Sea Sparrow Mk 3 SAM launchers; one 5in (127mm) gun; one Mk 10 Limbo A/S mortar; two triple Mk 32 torpedo tubes.
Propulsion: Two Pratt & Whitney FT4A2 gas turbines (50,000shp), two Pratt & Whitney FT12A3 gas turbines (7400shp); two shafts; 29+kts.

For many years the Royal Canadian Navy relied on British designs for its destroyers and frigates (which were built in Canadian yards), but in 1951 they decided to design their own. The result has been a series of unusual looking ships, packed with innovations, and ideally suited·to their role in the frequently inhospitable waters of the North Atlantic.

First was the *St Laurent* class of 2260 tons, whose six ships were commissioned in 1956-57. Three underwent a major refit in 1977-78 and the remainder in 1978-79, and all are due to be replaced by a new class in 1985-86. Next into service was the *Restigouche* class of three ships and the 'Improved Restigouche' (four ships). The latter class are armed with Sea Sparrow SAM, two 3in (76mm) guns and ASROC.

The design was further developed into the *Mackenzie* class (four ships) and the *Annapolis* class (two ships) which were commissioned 1962-64.

In the early 1970s the *DD 280* class appeared (*Iroquois, Huron, Athabaskan, Algonquin*). Like, their predecessors these have a distinctive appearance, albeit in a different way, with the high bridge and hangar interrupted by a lattice mast and a bifurcated funnel. The RCN has always

Below: HMCNS *Iroquois* (DD 280) with one of her two CHSS-2 Sea King helicopters coming in to land. The deckhouse before the bridge houses the launcher for the Canadian Sea Sparrow SAMs.

Above: HCMNS *Iroquois* (DD 280) firing a Canadian Sea Sparrow SAM. As with previous Canadian designs the DD 280s have a unique appearance with their high bridge and 'Y'-Shaped funnel.

used larger helicopters in relation to ship size than other navies and the *DD 280s* carry two Sea Kings. Landing is assisted by the 'Beartrap', a cable device which is attached to the hovering helicopter and which then hauls the aircraft onto the deck.

The new class of destroyers (due in 1985) must be awaited with interest, for Canadian designers will doubtless have a few more surprises for the naval world.

Hainan Class

Fast attack craft—patrol
25 craft.

Country of origin: China.
Displacement: 400 tons full load.
Dimensions: *Hull:* length overall 197ft (60m); beam 24ft (7·4m); draught 6·1ft (2·1m).
Armament: Two twin 57mm guns (fore and aft); four 25mm guns (twins); four MBU-1800 anti-submarine rocket launchers.
Propulsion: Diesels (8,000shp), two shafts; 28kts.

The USSR built some 150 *SO1* class large patrol craft in the late 1950s and 1960s some of which went to the PRC. Following the split between the two countries the PLA-Navy started producing its own designs which, for ease of production, were based on Soviet craft already in service. One of these was the *SO1*, which was lengthened and modified in minor ways to produce the *Hainan* class, production of which started in about 1964 and continues at a rate of four per year. There are two twin 57mm mounts and two twin 25mm together with four MBU-1800 anti-submarine rocket launchers.

The PLA-Navy's inventory must start an updating process soon, as nearly all the designs date back to the early 1950s. One new ship has been seen—the *Hai Dau* class, a 300 ton, missile-armed fast patrol boat, thought to be gas-turbine powered.

Above: A flotilla of *Hainan* class fast patrol craft off the Chinese coast. Of 400 tons full load displacement, these craft are designed in the PRC and are still being built at a rate of four per year. The weapon is an MBU-1800 four-barrel anti-submarine rocket launcher.

Left: *Hainan* class patrol craft on a firing exercise. All recent visitors to the PRC attest the very high standards maintained by the PLA-Navy: the ships and men are always extremely smart and the ships are in excellent condition. It is of interest that throughout the upheavals of the 1960s the PLA-Navy retained the traditional sailors' and officers' uniforms.

Luta Class

Guided missile destroyers
Seven+ ships including *No 240; No 241*

Country of origin: China.
Displacement: 3250 tons (3750 full load).
Dimensions: Length overall 430ft (131m); beam 45ft (13·7m); draught 15ft (4·6m).
Armament: Two triple SS-N-2 SSM launchers; four 130mm guns in two twin mounts, four 57mm AA guns, eight 25mm AA guns.
Propulsion: Geared turbines (45,000shp), twin shafts; 32+kts.

The Chinese Navy is now one of the most powerful in the Far East. Its first equipment after the People's Republic was set up in 1949 was ships captured from the Nationalists. These were a mixture of World War II Japanese, British and American designs. The seagoing vessels had mostly been transferred since 1945, and there was also a large number of river gunboats, some of which have actually been built for China. Russia soon

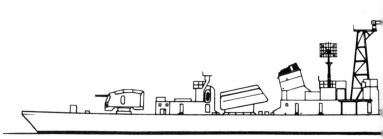

Above: The *Luta* class are the first major warships to be designed and built in PRC shipyards. They are based on the Soviet *Kotlin*, but with better armament, although the engines are less powerful.

supplied a number of World War II vessels to power this motley force, including four *Gordi* class destroyers and seven submarines. These were followed by four *Riga* class frigates, several *Whisky* class submarines and a number of guided-missile and patrol boats. Despite the political breach with Russia after 1956, the Chinese have built a number of modern warships to Russian designs, including *Golf, Romeo* and *Whisky* class submarines. The parts for some of these have been supplied from Russia, but others have been built entirely in Chinese yards. The Chinese have also produced modified versions of Russian designs. A number of modified *Riga* class frigates, *Kiangnans*, have been built since 1968, and the largest Chinese surface warships, the *Lutas*, are modified Russian *Kotlin* class destroyers. They have less powerful machinery than the *Kotlins*, and carry SSM launchers between and abaft the funnels in place of the *Kotlins'* torpedo tubes. These missiles are SSN-2 'Styx' SSMs and although they are obsolescent, they are still effective against any ship not equipped with modern ECM. The *Lutas* are much more effectively armed than the original Russian *Kildins*. These were modified *Kotlins* which carried a single SSN-1 'Scrubber' SSM launcher in place of the aft 5·1in (130mm) mount. However, the *Kildins* have since been rearmed with a much improved anti-aircraft armament and four SSN-2 (mod) SSM launchers, and are now better armed than the *Lutas*.

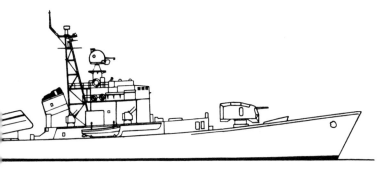

Below: *Luta* class destroyer at sea. The PRC Navy is the most numerous in the Far East, but its ships lack the sophisticated missiles and electronics needed for contemporary war at sea.

Shanghai Class

Fast attack craft

350+ craft: *Types I and II.*

Country of origin: China.
Displacement: 120 tons (155 full load).
Dimensions: Length overall 128ft (39m); beam 18ft (5·5m); draught 5·6ft (1·7m).
Armament: Four 37mm guns in two twin mounts, four 25mm automatic cannon in two twin mounts; *Shanghai I* has one twin 57mm mounting and one twin 18in torpedo tube; some craft have been seen with twin 18in recoilless rifle forward.
Propulsion: Four diesels, 4800bhp; 30kts.

The Chinese Navy now possesses the largest force of light craft in the world. It operates Russian and Chinese versions of a number of Russian designs, including *Osa* and *Komar* class guided-missile patrol boats and *P6* class torpedo boats. It also operates the Chinese-designed *Huchwan* class hydrofoils. However, over a third of its light craft are various types of *Shanghai* class patrol boat. These are conventional general purpose craft, similar in many ways to the larger Russian *SO1* class, a modified version of which is built in China as the *Hainan* class. The *Shanghais* are mainly intended for coastal patrol work, and have a powerful armament of light

Above: *Shanghai II* is armed with four 37mm and four 25mm cannon.

weapons. The initial boats differ from the later types by not having a twin 25mm mount immediately abaft the bridge. Some have an extra twin 37mm mount, and differ mainly from one another by the outline of their bridges. *Shanghais* have been supplied to many other countries, and a number of North Vietnamese boats were sunk by American ships and aircraft. The Romanians have given their *Shanghais* an increased armament, and have also built their own modified version.

Below: The *Shanghai* is numerically the largest single warship class in the world, with 350 serving with the Chinese PLA-Navy and about 100 in service with other countries. These 155 ton vessels are constructed at a rate of about ten a year and are armed with four 37mm twin guns and four 25mm cannon.

Clemenceau Class

Aircraft carriers

Two ships: *Clemenceau* (R-98); *Foch* (R-99).

Country of origin: France.
Displacement: 27,307 tons (32,780 full load).
Dimensions: Length overall 869·4ft (265m); width over flight deck 168ft (51·2m); draught 28·2ft (8·6m).
Aircraft: Typically, 20 Etendard, 10 Alize, 2 Super Frelon, 2 Alouette III.
Armament: Eight 3·9in (100mm) dual purpose guns in single mounts.
Propulsion: Two sets Parsons geared turbines (126,000shp), two shafts; 32kts.

After World War II *Bearn* was totally obsolete, and the French naval air arm was reformed round the escort carrier *Dixmude* (ex-*Biter*, ex-*Rio Parana*). Transferred in 1945, she was used operationally in French Indo-China, but was later reduced to an aircraft transport and then a barracks. She was returned to the USA in 1965 and sunk as a target. *Dixmude* was supplemented by *Arromanches* (R-95, ex-*Colossus*). This ex-British light fleet carrier was similar to the *Colossus* and *Majestic* class light fleet carriers transferred or sold to Argentina, Australia, Brazil, Canada, India and the Netherlands. She was originally lent for five years from August 1946, but was purchased by France after a refit in 1951. She was rebuilt with a 4° angle deck and mirror landing sight in 1957 — 1959 to operate modern anti-submarine aircraft and was not discarded until the early 1970s. To fill the gap before the French built their own aircraft-carriers, two American light carriers, *Belleau Wood* (renamed *Bois Belleau)* and *Langley* (renamed *Lafayette*) were transferred in 1951. They were returned to the USA in 1960 and 1963 respectively, as the new *Clemenceau* became ready for service. The latter are the first aircraft-carriers designed and built as such to be completed in France. The first French post-war design, prepared in 1947, was for a 16,000 ton (16,260 tonne) light carrier, but this project was abandoned, and the *Clemenceaus* are much larger ships. They are similar in size to the American *Essex* class, which they resemble in many respects, but ▶

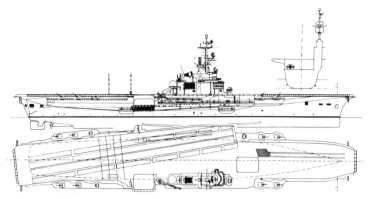

Above: *Clemenceau* class, France's first purpose-built carriers.

Above: A Dassault Etendard IVM strike aircraft lands on the angled deck of the *Clemenceau* (R-98) during an exercise.

Clemenceau at sea with her aircraft complement parked on the flight-deck. Visible are Vought F-8E(FN) Crusaders (now retired), Etendard fighters, and Breguet Alize ASW aircraft.

Clemenceau (R-98) at sea. There are two carriers of this class, and the other one—*Foch* (R-99)—carries only helicopters in an ASW role. These two ships were the first aircraft carriers to be designed and built in France and were commissioned in 1961 and 1963. The next French carrier will be nuclear-powered (PA-75) and will operate fixed-wing V/STOL aircraft of unspecified type.

they have a stern similar to the later British carriers. They were designed to carry a powerful gun anti-aircraft armament which, unusually, they still retain. They were originally to have been armed with 12 twin 57mm guns. This was altered to 12 single 3·9in (100mm) guns in 1956, and was fixed at eight 3·9in (100mm) guns in 1958. They were completed with an armoured 8° angled flight deck, a mirror landing sight designed in France, two lifts and two steam catapults. They have one hangar deck. The funnel is blended in with the island superstructure, as in American carriers. They are fitted with the DRB1 10 three-dimensional radar and SENIT tactical data system, which is based on US equipment. They also have an SOS-505 sonar. The *Clemenceaus* are too small to operate large modern carrier aircraft, and too much may have been attempted on too limited a displacement. *Clemenceau* was fitted with bulges after trials and *Foch* received hers during construction. Nevertheless, they give France a more powerful carrier attack force than any country except USA and USSR. A 30,000 ton (30,480 tonne) carrier was projected in the 1958 estimates, but was cancelled because of financial economies. A nuclear-powered helicopter carrier (PA-75) is at present projected. This is comparable in all but machinery with the British *Invincible* (CAH-1), and will have an uninterrupted flight deck and hangar capable of operating either ten to fifteen large or 25 small helicopters, or a mix of helicopters and V/STOL aircraft. As a peacetime economy measure *Clemenceau* operates fixed wing aircraft, while *Foch* operates only helicopters in the anti-submarine role.

Below: Etendard IVMs above *Clemenceau*. They will be replaced in the near future by the much improved Super Etendard.

Above: The aircraft carrier *Foch* (R-99) is limited to rotary-winged aircraft like these Aerospatiale Super Frelons.

19

Daphne Class

Patrol Submarines
9 boats including *Daphne* (S641), *Sirene* (S-651).

Country of origin: France.
Displacement: 869 tons surfaced; 1043 tons submerged.
Dimensions: Length overall 189·6ft (57·8m); beam 22·3ft (6·8m); draught 15·1ft (4·6m).
Armament: 12 21·7in (550mm) torpedo tubes.
Propulsion: SEMT-Pielstick diesel-electric 16bhp, two shafts; 13·5kts surfaced, 16kts submerged.

In the three years following the Liberation the French Navy had up to fourteen different types of submarine in service, ranging in size from ocean-going types to 'midget submarines'. The first submarines to be constructed after the war were improved versions of the German Type XXI, one of which, U-2518, had been taken over by the French in 1945 and renamed *Roland Morillot* (S-613). Six of these new vessels were built as the *Narval* class and all are still in service, all of them having been built in the early 1950s and rebuilt in the late 1960s. These boats displace 1910 tons submerged, have six 21·7in (550mm) torpedo tubes, and have speeds of 15 knots surfaced and 18 knots dived.

The next class to appear was the *Arethuse*, small 669 ton (submerged) hunter/killers, of which four were built between 1955 and 1958. All four are still in service, armed with four automatically homing torpedoes.

Following from the success of the *Arethuse* class the French produced a somewhat enlarged version, displacing 1,043 tons submerged, designated the *Daphne* class. Very careful attention was paid to silence of operation; the exterior shape of the hull was tank-tested in great detail and all mooring equipment is retractable. There are even microphones around the hull which enable those inside to monitor noise-levels and to regulate speed or manoeuvre accordingly.

The *Daphne* class boats were an immediate success and eleven entered service with the French Navy between 1964 and 1970. In addition, 10 were sold overseas (South Africa 3, Pakistan 3, Portugal 4) and four were constructed in Spain. In 1968, however, *Minerve* disappeared without

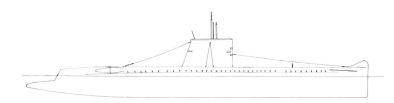

Above: The *Daphne* class. An efficient, conventional hunter/killer.

Above: The *Daphne* (S-641). Note the exceptionally clean lines and the smooth deck, which contribute to the silent operation.

trace in the Mediterranean, followed in 1970 by *Eurydice*. These two mysterious and worrying incidents were followed in early 1971 by the *Flore*, when the schnorkel sprang a leak due to a faulty valve, but on this occasion the captain took rapid remedial action and managed to save his submarine. Although there have been no more losses there have been no more sales either. The *Daphne* class was succeeded by the *Agosta* class (four built) and a nuclear class is planned.

Below: Patrol submarine *Daphne* (S-641) at sea in the Mediterranean. Two of this class disappeared without trace in 1968 and 1970, but the fault was found when a third boat was just saved.

D'Estienne d'Orves Class

Frigates

13 ships including *D'Estienne d'Orves* (F-781); *Amyot d'Inville* (F-782).

Country of origin: France.
Displacement: 950 tons (1170 full load).
Dimensions: Length overall 249·3ft (76m); beam 33·8ft (10·3m); draught 9·8ft (3m).
Armament: One 3·9in (100mm) main gun, two 20mm AA guns; all ships fitted for two Exocet SSM launchers, but only those deployed overseas will actually mount missiles.
Propulsion: Two SEMT-Pielstick diesels (11,000bhp), two shafts; 24kts.

The French built 18 *Le Corse* (type E-50) and *Le Normand* (Type E-52) class seagoing fast escorts between 1951 and 1960. They had a speed of 28kts, a standard displacement of about 1,290 tons (1,310 tonnes) and an armament of three twin 57mm mounts and A/S weapons. They were steam-turbine powered and had a reasonable range. An enlarged class, the *Commandant Rivères* (Type E-55), which are diesel powered with a speed of 25kts and armed with three single 3·9in (100mm) guns and A/S weapons, were built between 1957 and 1965. They can carry two landing craft and an 80-man commando unit for operations in French possessions

Above: *D'Estienne d'Orves.* Note Exocet launchers beside funnel.

abroad. They are being refitted with four MM-38 Exocet SSMs in place of B mount. The *D'Estienne d'Orves* are smaller, more specialised vessels with a very limited anti-aircraft armament and are mainly intended for anti-submarine operations in coastal waters, though they can also be used for service overseas. The single 3.9in (100mm) gun is mounted forward, immediately ahead of the large bridge and the 14.8in (375mm) A/S rocket launcher is mounted on the deckhouse aft. Those vessels used overseas can mount an MM-38 Exocet SSM on either side of the funnel to confer some independent offensive capability, but this design is mainly dependent on other vessels or aircraft for protection against a serious threat from surface warships or aircraft. However, these relatively cheap and unsophisticated vessels can be built in greater numbers than the much larger missile and helicopter-armed *Georges Leygues* class (Type C-70).

Left: An Exocet MM-38 SSM is fired from a frigate of the *D'Estienne d'Orves* class.

Below: *Detroyat* (F-784), the fourth in a class of thirteen cost-effective frigates.

Bottom: *Drogou* (F-783). Note Exocet and different radar compared to *Detroyat*.

Le Redoutable

Nuclear-powered ballistic missile submarines

Five boats: *Le Redoutable* (S-611); *Le Terrible* (S-612); *Le Foudroyant* (S-610); *L'Indomptable* (S-613); *Le Tonnant* (S-614).

Country of origin: France.
Displacement: 7500 tons surfaced (9000 tons submerged).
Dimensions: Length overall 420ft (128m); beam 34.8ft (10.6m); draught 32.8ft (10m).
Armament: 16 MSBS M-2 missiles (M-20 in *L'Indomptable* and *Le Terrible*); four 21.7in (550mm) torpedo tubes.
Propulsion: One pressurised water-cooled reactor, two turbo-alternators, one electric motor (15,000shp), one shaft; 25kts submerged; also one reserve diesel engine (2670shp).

Below: The French nuclear-powered ballistic missile submarine
Le Redoutable (S-611) at sea. The existence of a second
European independent nuclear force adds greatly to the deterrent.

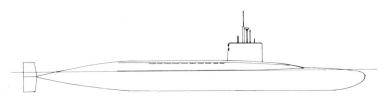

Above: *Le Redoutable* **class; five boats are now operational.**

Like Britain, France decided to build nuclear ballistic missile submarines to ensure a viable nuclear deterrent, but unlike the British Polaris submarines, the French *'Force de dissuasion'* was developed completely independently of the United States. This resulted in a much greater effort spread over a longer timescale (the French are only now able to start their nuclear attack submarine building programme) and in heavier missiles than Polaris carrying a smaller warhead over a shorter range. The MSBS-M1 SLBM fitted in the first two boats has a range of 1,300 miles (1,000nm). *Le Foudroyant* carries the improved M2 SLBM, which is also being retrofitted in *Le Redoutable*, and the M-20 SLBM can be fitted in *L'Indomptable*. This has a thermonuclear reinforced warhead and has a range of about 1,500 nautical miles. An ▶

enlarged version, the M4 SLBM, with a MIRV warhead, was tested in 1978–1979 in the experimental diesel-electric submarine *Gymnote* (S-655), which has been used to develop the *Le Redoutables* and their missiles. It was built between 1963 and 1966, and has two SLBM launching tubes and laboratories. The *Le Redoutables* resemble the American nuclear ballistic missile submarines, with two rows of eight vertical SLBM launching tubes abaft the fin, which carries the forward hydroplanes. Possibly reflecting doubts about the reliability of their nuclear reactor, the *Le Redoutables* have turbo-electric propulsion with an auxiliary diesel that can be cut in to provide power and propulsion in the event of a reactor failure. An order was placed in late 1978 for a sixth SSBN of a more advanced design. This boat, *L'Inflexible*, will enter service in 1985, and all six boats will be replaced by a totally new class in 1990–2000.

Right: *Le Foudroyant* (S-610) heads out on patrol. The French, unlike the British, have built five SSBNs, thus guaranteeing one boat at sea at all times.

Below: The realisation of a national dream as the first French nuclear submarine is launched by President de Gaulle (29 Mar 75).

Bottom: *Le Redoutable* during her sea trials off Cherbourg on 25 June 1973. A sixth boat will be laid down in 1980.

Suffren Class

Guided missile destroyers
Two ships: *Suffren* (D-602); *Duquesne* (D-603).

Country of origin: France.
Displacement: 5090 tons (6090 full load).
Dimensions: Length overall 517·1ft (157·6m), beam 50·9ft (15·5m), draught 20ft (6·1m).
Armament: Four Exocet SSM launchers, twin Masurca SAM launcher, one Malafor AS missile launcher; two 3·9in (100mm) main guns, two 20mm AA guns; four launchers for AS homing torpedoes.
Propulsion: Rateau geared turbines (72,500shp), twin shafts; 34kts.

The *Suffrens* (F-60 Type) are the first of a new generation of French warships, and are also the first French purpose-built guided-missile destroyers. They mount two single 3·9in (100mm) guns in the bows, the Malafon ASM launcher is immediately abaft the prominent mack, and the Masurca SAM launcher is on the quarter-deck with variable depth sonar at the stern. There are four Exocets in place of one 100mm gun in *Duquesne*. These ships are easily recognisable by their enormous glass fibre domes on the top of the bridge which carry DRB1 23 three-dimensional radar. The Dutch *Tromp* class guided-missile destroyers, which also have a large dome on the bridge, have a much bulkier silhouette. The *Suffrens* are excellent seaboats, and make an interesting comparison with the British *County* class

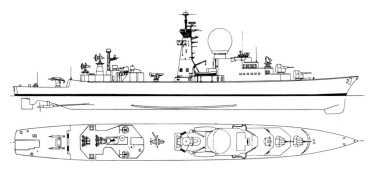

Above: Two of these 6,000 ton *Suffren* class destroyers were built.

guided-missile destroyers. The latter have two close-range Sea Cat SAM launchers and a helicopter pad and hangar, whereas the French ships have two tracking radars for their single SAM system, A/S torpedo tubes, a long-range ASM launcher and variable depth sonar. The British adopted COSAG machinery, whilst the French, who were the first major Western power to adopt an operational SSM, stuck to steam turbines until gas turbine power had been proved by other countries. The *Tourville* class (F-67 Type) combine

Below: The *Suffren* (D-602) in the Mediterranean. The enormous radome houses the DRBI-23 three-dimensional radar for air search and target designation for the Masurca air defence weapons system.

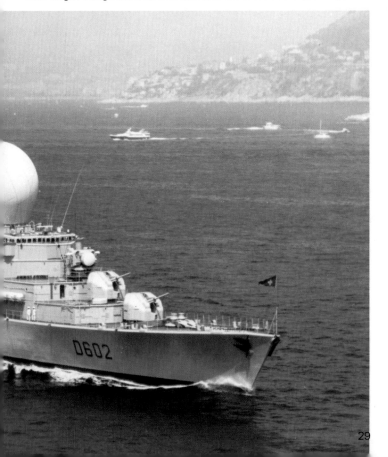

the best features from this design with that of the smaller anti-submarine *Aconit* (D-609) (C-65 Type). They are turbine powered and carry MM-38 Exocet SSMs and a helicopter pad and hangar in place of the Masurca SAM. The *Tourvilles* have themselves been replaced by the *Aconit*-sized *Georges Leygués* class (C-70 Type) powered by gas turbines and diesels. The Malafon ASMs on the *Suffrens* provide long distance A/S defence, and mean that a helicopter, with its associated pad and hangar need not be carried. The use of a Mack has also increased the available deck space for other weapons systems. A comprehensive selection of radar and ECM

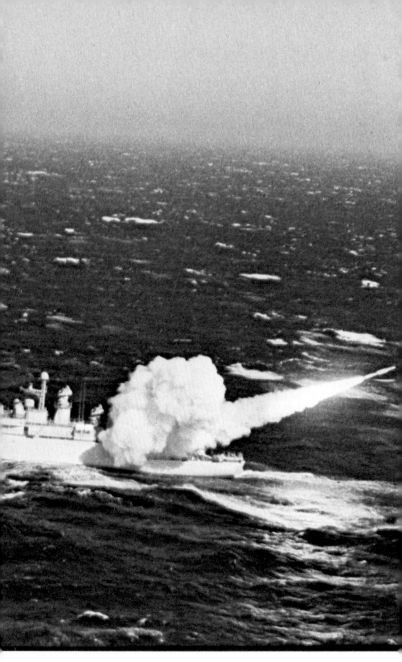

The *Suffren* class destroyers are larger than the Soviet *Kynda* class cruisers; they are handsome, well-designed ships with excellent stability which makes them good weapons platforms.

aerials are carried on the fore part and top of the Mack. Although they carry a smaller crew for their size than earlier vessels, later French ships are more automated and need an even smaller crew. Personnel costs are of major importance to modern navies, and so every effort is made to make ships and their associated weapons systems as automated as possible.

Hamburg Class

Destroyers

Four ships: *Hamburg* (D-181); *Schleswig-Holstein* (D 182); *Bayern* (D- 183); *Hessen* (D-184).

Country of origin: Federal Republic of Germany.
Displacement: 3340 tons (4692 full load).
Dimensions: Length overall 439·7ft (134m); beam 44ft (13·4m); draught 15·7ft (4·8m).
Armament: Four Exocet SSM launchers; three 3·9in (100mm) main guns in single mounts, four twin 40mm AA guns; four 21in torpedo tubes.
Propulsion: Two Wahoday geared turbines, twin shafts, 68,000shp; 34kts.

Unlike the interwar German Navy, which had at least had some continuity with its predecessor, the Federal German Navy was forced to rebuild virtually from scratch. The first requirement was for light craft, but larger vessels were soon required. The first major units were the *Köln* class frigates, but after the Federal Navy had been permitted to exceed the 3,000 ton (3,048t) limit that had been imposed on it after World War II, and had laid down the 4,880 ton (4,958t) armed training vessel *Deutschland*, the way was open to build the *Hamburg* class destroyers.

They have the piled-up look typical of all modern German warships, with a relatively low freeboard and the guns mounted near the ends of the ship. The *Hamburgs* are designed for the Baltic, where seaworthiness is less important than a powerful AA armament, high speed and manoeuvrability. They can carry mines, a useful weapon in the shallow Baltic, but do not operate helicopters because all the likely operational areas can be covered by land-based aircraft. The greatest weakness in the original design was the lack of a weapon capable of dealing with a major surface warship, so the class has been fitted with four Exocet SSMs in place of X mounting.

Below: The *Hamburg* class is designed for the Baltic. It does not operate helicopters as land-based aircraft are always in range.

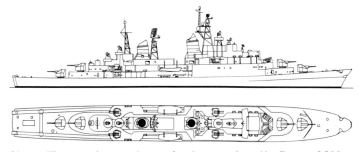

Above: The superimposed turret has been replaced by Exocet SSMs.

Above: Like so many German ships the *Hamburg* class appears top-heavy, with a massive superstructure on a low freeboard hull.

Köln Class

Frigates

Six ships including *Köln* (F-220); *Augsburg* (F-222).

Country of origin: Federal Republic of Germany.
Displacement: 2100 tons (2550 full load).
Dimensions: 360.9ft (110m); beam 36.1ft (11m); draught 11.2ft (3.4m).
Armament: Two 3.9in (100mm) main guns; two twin, two single 40mm AA guns; four 21in torpedo tubes.
Propulsion: Four MAN diesels, 12,000bhp; two Brown Boveri gas turbines, 24,000bhp; twin shafts; 32kts.

Köln (F-220) was the first escort to be built in Germany after World War II, and entered service in April 1961. Designed mainly for use in the Baltic, the *Köln* class, like most modern Baltic warships, concentrate on speed and a powerful anti-aircraft armament rather than range and seaworthiness. In common with the *Hamburg* class destroyers, they have a low flush-deck hull and a piled-up superstructure. The French-designed automatic 3.9in (100mm) guns are arranged in two single mounts, one at either end of the ship. There is a twin 40mm mount in B and X position, and a single 40mm gun on either side of the superstructure aft. The two Bofors A/S rocket-launchers are mounted side-by-side between the forward 40mm mount and the open bridge. There are prominent air intakes for the gas turbines on either side of the bridge and the large, lipped funnel makes the class easy to identify. The CODAG machinery consists of two diesels and one gas turbine coupled to each shaft with controllable pitch propellers. The radar is Dutch, but the ships have German hull-mounted sonar. The class was refitted and modernised from 1967. They still lack a medium or close-range anti-aircraft missile, and it was intended to build a developed version displacing 3,200 tons (3,250 tonnes) standard, armed with two 3in (76mm) guns and a single Tartar SAM. This was the Type 121 Frigate 70 design, but it has now been discarded in favour of building 12 Type 122 frigates, based on the Dutch *Kortenaer* design. Slightly larger than the Type 121, these will have Harpoon SSMs and Sea Sparrow SAMs, as well as guns and A/S weapons and two helicopters.

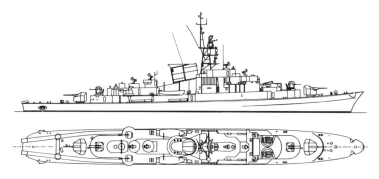

Above: This ship has the same 'piled-up' appearance as the *Hamburg*.

Above: The six *Köln* class frigates are due to be replaced in the 1980s by a new class based on the Dutch *Kortenaer* design.

GNS Köln (F-220) leaving harbour. Although heavily armed for the size of hull, these ships have a limited range (920 miles at 32 knots) due to the particular requirements of Baltic service.

Type 143 Class

Guided missile patrol boats
10 ships: P-6111 - P-6120.

Country of origin: Federal Republic of Germany.
Displacement: 295 tons (378 full load).
Dimensions: Length overall 188.6ft (57.5m); beam 24.9ft (7.6m); draught 9.2ft (2.8m).
Armament: Two 3in (76mm) guns in single mounts; four Exocet SSM launchers; two 21in torpedo tubes.
Propulsion: Four MTU diesels (16,000bhp), four shafts; 38kts.

Lürssen, the designers of the World War II *Schnellboote*, built a number of modified versions for the German Navy and for export after the war. These were eventually developed into the Type 141 and Type 142 torpedo boats, built between 1957 and 1963. Meanwhile Lürssen had developed a general-purpose hull that could be fitted with a variety of engines and armaments depending on the requirements of the purchasing navy. For political reasons this was transferred to France, where it was lengthened and modified and became *La Combattante*. A scaled-up version of this type was chosen to form the basis of a missile-armed patrol boat for the Federal German Navy, which became the Type 143. These boats are intended to operate in the Baltic, so have a high speed and are fitted with an OTO Melara 3in (76mm) Compact mount fore and aft to ensure adequate anti-aircraft protection. They have AG15 automatic data link with their shore base (which can fire and control their MM-38 Exocet SSMs) and they have Dutch tracking radar. The Type 143s also carry two torpedo tubes firing Seal wire-guided torpedoes with a range of about 22,000 yards (20,000m). The French variant of this design (known as the *Combattante III* type) is being built for Greece, and Spain and Turkey have similar Lürssen-designed boats. The Israeli *Reshef* class (also building for South Africa) is also very similar. The types and mix of guns and missiles, and the power required, vary from country to country. Twenty of the smaller *Combattante II* type, the Type 148, have been built for Germany between 1972 and 1975. They also have AG15 and Exocet SSMs.

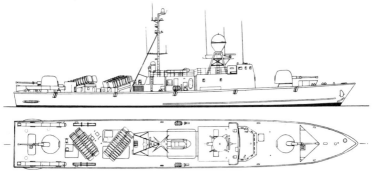

Above: The angled launchers for Exocet SSMs are clearly shown.

Above: Seen on the stern of this Type 143 are the tubes for the 'Seal' 21in(533mm) wire-guided torpedoes.

Left: Main armament of the Type 143 is four Exocet SSM and two Oto Melara 3in (76mm) guns. Radar is by Hollandse.

Below: P-6114 at speed; four MTU diesels give a maximum speed of 38 knots on 16000 bhp.

Dolfijn Class

Submarines

Four boats: *Dolfijn; Zeehond; Potvis; Tonijn.*

Country of origin: Netherlands
Displacement: 1494 tons surfaced (1826 tons submerged).
Dimensions: Length overall 260.9ft (79.5m); beam 25.8ft (7.8m); draught 16.4ft (5m).
Armament: Eight 21in (533mm) torpedo tubes.
Propulsion: Two MAN diesels (3100hp), electric motors (4200hp); twin shafts; 14.5kts surfaced (17kts submerged).

These four submarines were originally ordered together. *Potvis* and *Tonijn* were then delayed for several years and their equipment differed somewhat from the first two when they finally entered service. However, all four submarines have since been refitted to a virtually identical standard. The outstanding feature of this class is that instead of having the usual single pressure hull of a normal submarine, they have three separate though interconnected pressure hulls in a 'treble bubble' arrangement. The uppermost and largest contains the crew and most of the equipment, whilst below it and alongside each other are two smaller hulls, each containing machinery and stores. The advantage of this odd layout is that it gives increased strength and compactness. However, the lower two hulls are extremely cramped, making machinery maintenance and replacement very difficult. This, combined with the increased complexity and therefore increased manufacturing cost, would appear to have stopped the Dutch from developing the design further. Their latest submarines have reverted to the conventional single pressure hull arrangement. However, the triple hull arrangement has allowed a designed diving depth of 980ft (300m). The streamlined hull gives an excellent performance submerged and they are very quiet boats.

Above: The *Dolfijn* class submarine *Potvis*. These boats have three pressure hulls, housing crew and armament, batteries, and diesels respectively. Commissioned 1961-65, they are very quiet boats.

Below: *Potvis* (S-804). These four boats were originally in two separate classes, but as a result of modernisation they are now virtually identical and regarded as one class.

Kortenaer Class

Frigates
19 ships under construction and more planned.

Country of origin: Netherlands.
Displacement: 3500 tons.
Dimensions: Length overall 419·8ft (128m); beam 47·2ft (14·4m); draught 14·3ft (4·4m).
Aircraft: Two Westland Lynx helicopters (one only in peace).
Armament: Two quadruple Harpoon SSM launchers, one octuple Sea Sparrow SAM launcher; two single 76mm guns (see text); two double tubes for Mk46 torpedoes.
Propulsion: Two Rolls Royce Olympus gas turbines. (50,000shp), two Rolls Royce Olympus gas turbines (8000shp), twin shafts; 30kts.

The Dutch Navy is undertaking a fundamental reorganisation over the years 1975-83 with the aim of creating an integrated, efficient and balanced force. At the heart of this plan is the creation of three task forces, each comprising a flagship, six ASW frigates and a logistic support vessel; two of these task forces will be allocated to CINCEASTLANT and the third to CINCHAN. The 18 ASW frigates will be found from the six *Van Speijk* class (modified, Dutch-built versions of the British *Leander* class) and the remaining 12 will be the new *Kortenaer* class. The *Tromp* class destroyers will provide two of the flagships, but the third will be a modified *Kortenaer*, bringing the total Dutch order for these ships to 13.

The West German Navy needs to replace its four ex-US Navy *Fletcher* class destroyers and its six *Köln* class frigates in the mid-eighties and this is to be achieved by building a modified version of *Kortenaer* for service in the Baltic. Six are already ordered, with a possibility of a further eight to follow. Thus, with 19 being built and more in prospect the *Kortenaer* is a most

important ship in the NATO inventory. These ships represent a fine balance between heavy armament and economy in manpower. There is one 76mm gun mounted forward, a Sea Sparrow launcher, two Harpoon launchers amidships and four torpedo tubes. A point defence system is to be mounted on the hangar roof; a second 76mm gun is fitted in the first two ships and the next ten will have a rapid firing light gun such as the Oerlikon/Oto 35mm, but the final system may be the Signaal GOALKEEPER. The hangar can accommodate two Lynxes, but only one is carried in peacetime. All this is achieved with a complement of 196—a most creditable accomplishment.

Above: The Dutch frigate *Kortenaer*; 13 are already on order for the Dutch Navy and a further six for the West German Navy.

Below: Main armament of the *Kortenaer* class are eight Harpoon SSMs, two 76mm guns, Sea Sparrow BPDMS and two Westland Lynx helicopters.

Tromp Class

Guided missile destroyers

Two ships: *Tromp* (F-801); *De Ruyter* (ex-*Heemskerke*, F-806).

Country of origin: Netherlands.
Displacement: 4300 tons (5400 full load).
Dimensions: Length overall 454.1ft (138.4m); beam 48.6ft (14.8m); draught 15.1ft (4.6m).
Aircraft: One Westland Lynx helicopter.
Armament: Eight Harpoon SSM launchers, one Tartar Mk 13 SAM launcher, two quad Sea Sparrow SAM Launchers; two 4.7in (120mm) guns in twin turret; two triple Mk32 ASW torpedo tubes.
Propulsion: Two Rolls Royce Olympus gas turbines (50,000shp); two Rolls Royce Tyne cruising gas turbines (8000shp); twin shafts; 30kts.

These ships are the equivalent of the Canadian *Iroquois*, the French *Georges Leygues*, the British *Sheffield* and Italian *Audace* classes. They are fitted with eight Harpoon SSMs between the bridge and funnels, and are among the best ships of their type. The 4.7in (120mm) twin mountings come from scrapped *Holland* class destroyers, but have been thoroughly modernised. The short-range Sea Sparrow BPDMS mounting is fitted in B position. Behind it is a massive bridge, surmounted by a Dutch 3-D radar in a large glass-fibre dome. The uptakes are splayed out in a similar way to the Canadian *Iroquois* class to keep the exhaust clear of the radars. The Standard Tartar Mk 13 SAM launcher is aft, just forward of the hangar and flight deck for a Lynx A/S helicopter.

Triple Mk 32 torpedo tubes are mounted either side of the aft superstructure. The *Tromps* have COGOG machinery, the Olympuses giving full speed and the Tynes cruising. They have controllable-pitch propellers. These ships are intended for the European theatre, and are well balanced vessels capable of dealing with air, surface and underwater threats. The *Tromps* replace the *De Zeven Provincien* class light cruisers, and these highly effective vessels save considerably in manpower.

Above: *Tromp* (F-801). Note the twin 4.7in(120mm) turret on the foredeck, with the Sea Sparrow SAM launcher immediately behind. The huge radome houses the Hollandse Signaalapparaten 3-dimension Multi-Target Tracking Radar; the unofficial name is 'Kojak class'.

Below: *Tromp* class. Harpoon SSM launchers have been fitted just forward of the funnel since this picture was taken. Note also the Tartar SAM launcher atop the helicopter hangar and the landing deck aft. Two of this very efficient design were built.

Andrea Doria Class and Vittorio Veneto Class

Escort cruisers
Three ships: *Andrea Doria* (C-553); *Caio Duilio* (C-554); *Vittorio Veneto* (C-550).

Andrea Doria class:
Country of origin: Italy.
Displacement: 5000 tons (6500 full load).
Dimensions: Length overall 489.8ft (149.3m); beam 56.4ft (17.2m); draught 16.4ft (5m).
Aircraft: Four Augusta-Bell 204B or 212 helicopters.
Armament: One twin Terrier SAM launcher (Standard SAM in *Andrea Doria*); eight 3in (76mm) guns in single mounts; two triple US Mk 32 torpedo tubes.
Propulsion: Two geared turbines (60,000shp), twin shaft; 31kts.
Vittorio Veneto class:
Country of origin: Italy.
Displacement: 7500 tons (8850 full load).
Dimensions: Length overall 589ft (179.6m); beam 63.6ft (19.4m); draught 19.7ft (6m).
Aircraft: Nine Augusta-Bell 204B or 212 helicopters.
Armament: One twin Terrier SAM launcher; eight 3in (76mm) guns in single mounts; two triple US Mk-32 torpedo tubes.
Propulsion: Two Tosi geared turbines (73,000shp), twin shaft; 32kts.

Below: *Andrea Doria* at sea with a Sikorsky S-58 on the flight-deck; normal complement is four Augusta-Bell 204B or 212. She was used for Harrier trials in 1969.

Above: *Andrea Doria* mounts Terrier SAMs and four helicopters.

The *Andrea Dorias* are the first of the modern escort cruisers, which can operate and maintain a number of A/S helicopters. They were evolved from the *Impavido* class destroyers, but are larger and beamier ships. They have a flush deck, and were designed round the ability to carry Terrier SAMs and four Agusta-Bell 204B A/S helicopters. The Terrier SAM twin-launcher is carried forward, and the 3in (76mm) AA single mounts are arranged around the slab-sided superstructure in lozenge fashion. They have unit machinery separated by living spaces, and the hangar is arranged around and abaft of the second funnel. The 98·5ft by 52·5ft (30m by 16m) flight deck is right aft, and is cantilevered out at the stern to ensure the maximum possible area for operating helicopters. *Andrea Doria* (C-553) was used for Harrier V/STOL aircraft handling trials in 1969 but she is too small to carry them operationally. They have SOS-23 hull-mounted sonar and two triple Mk 32 A/S torpedo tube mounts, one either side of the hangar. Although the *Andrea Dorias* are very useful ships, they are really too small to fulfil their designed role. Despite being stabilised (like almost all modern warships) a larger hull is necessary to operate helicopters safely in rough weather, and the hangar and flight deck are extremely cramped. They also lack any weapons capable of countering a major surface threat. However, they are intended to operate under friendly air cover and as part of a task force. *Andrea Doria* (C-553) ▶

was modernised 1976-1978 and was fitted for standard SAMs, which have a limited SSM capacity.

Two designs were proposed for improved *Andrea Dorias*. The first was for a large ship capable of being used for amphibious assault as well as for A/S work; in some ways she would have resembled the French *Jeanne d'Arc* (ex-*La Résolue*). She was originally to have been named *Italia*, though this was later changed to *Trieste*. This project was cancelled in 1968. The other project was for a larger *Andrea Doria*. This became *Vittorio Veneto* (C-550), and her design was considerably modified to take advantage of operational experience with the previous two ships. Like the *Andrea Dorias*, she has a twin-launcher forward, but this can fire ASROC ASMs as well as Terrier SAMs, thereby providing the ship with a self-contained long-range A/S system. She also has her 3in (76mm) AA guns arranged in lozenge fashion

Vittorio Veneto's design incorporates the lessons learnt with the two earlier ships, with better armament, more room, and more than twice the number of helicopters.

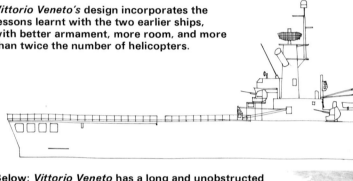

Below: Vittorio Veneto has a long and unobstructed flight-deck measuring 131ft x 60.6ft(40m x 18.5m) from which her squadron of nine Agusta-Bell 212 helicopters operates. There are two lifts to the hangar which is below the flight-deck. Vittorio Veneto is the largest surface ship in the Italian Navy and is the commander-in-chief's flagship.

round the superstructure but has macks instead of funnels. In order to carry more than twice the *Andrea Dorias'* number of helicopters, she has a raised quarterdeck over a hangar, which is served by two lifts. The flight deck measures 131ft by 60·6ft (40m by 18·5m), and the facilities for handling helicopters are much less cramped than on her predecessors. She is a very effective vessel, ideally suited for Mediterranean A/S warfare. Like the *Andrea Dorias,* she lacks a powerful surface weapon, but she, like them, is designed to operate as part of a task force. She is the largest warship in the Italian Navy and is used as the flagship. Several proposals have been made to build a larger version of *Vittorio Veneto* (C-550), but these have now been shelved in favour of a 'through-deck cruiser' design by Italcantieri. This ship, the *Giuseppe Garibaldi,* is a 12,000 ton (13,250 full load) aircraft carrier; she was laid down in 1979 and is due to join the fleet in 1982.

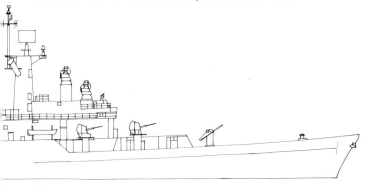

Above: *Vittorio Veneto* (C-550) at sea in the Mediterranean. The twin missile launcher forward can fire either *Terrier* SAMs or ASROC anti-submarine missiles, a most useful dual capability. Close-in air defence is provided by eight 3in(76mm) guns which encircle the superstructure. The next aircraft-carrier, the *Guiseppe Garibaldi,* will have a through-deck and a starboard island, and is due to join the fleet in 1982.

Audace Class

Destroyers
Two ships: *Audace* (D-551); *Ardito* (D-550).

Country of origin: Italy.
Displacement: 3600 tons (4400 full load).
Dimensions: Length overall 446·4ft (136·6m); beam 47·1ft (14·5m); draught 15ft (4·6m).
Aircraft: Two Agusta-Bell 204B or 212 helicopters.
Armament: One single Tartar/Standard Mk13 SAM launcher; two 5in (127mm), four 3in (76mm) guns, all in single mounts; two triple US Mk32 torpedo tubes.
Propulsion: Two sets geared turbines (73,000shp), twin shaft; 33kts.

The *Impetuoso* class, the first postwar destroyers to be designed and built in Italy, were ordered in 1950, and were strongly influenced by American designs. Flushdecked and twin-funnelled, they were armed with American guns and fitted with American radar and sonar. However, they were closely tailored to Mediterranean requirements. In addition to four 5in (127mm)

Below: *Audace* class. Two of these large, well armed destroyers have been built in Italy.

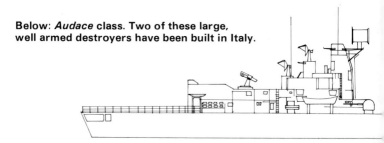

guns mounted in twin turrets fore and aft, they had a powerful anti-aircraft (16 × 40mm) and anti-submarine (Menon triple barrel mortar and ASW torpedo) armament and a high speed.

The next class, the *Impavidos* ordered in 1957 and 1959, were enlarged and improved versions with the aft 5in mount replaced by a single Mk 13 Tartar SAM launcher capable of launching Tartar or Standard missiles. There is magazine space for 40 missiles. The 40mm guns were replaced by the Italian Brescia 3in (76mm) gun. They have no hangar, but operate a single Agusta Bell 204B ASW helicopter from the stern. In the late 1960s, replacement of the *Impetuosos'* aft twin 5in mount with a single Tartar SAM launcher was considered but not carried out.

The *Audace* class is a further enlargement and development of the *Impavidos*. On a slightly larger hull, the American twin 5in mount is replaced by two single superimposed OTO Melara guns. The AA armament amidships is the 3in (76mm) OTO Melara Compact mount, and a hangar has been provided aft for two AB-204B or AB-212 helicopters, although these may be replaced by two Sikorsky SH-3D Sea Kings. The Mark 13 SAM launcher is mounted above the hangar and has a magazine capacity for 36 missiles. The ships have a comprehensive fit of US radar and Dutch sonar. Two 'Improved Audace' DDGs with either COGOG or CODOG machinery are planned, but a final decision has not yet been made.

Photo below: *Audace* (D-551). These ships can operate two Agusta-Bell 204B or one Sikorsky SH-3D Sea King anti-submarine warfare helicopters.

D 551

Enrico Toti Class

Submarines

Four boats: *Enrico Toti* (S-506); *Attitio Bagnolini* (S-505);
Enrico Dandolo (S-515); *Lazzaro Mocenigo* (S-514).

Country of origin: Italy.
Displacement: 524 tons surfaced (582 tons submerged).
Dimensions: Length overall 151·5ft (42·6m); beam 15·4ft (4·7m); draught 13·1ft (4m).
Armament: Four 21in (533mm) torpedo tubes.
Propulsion: Two Fiat diesels, one electric motor (2200shp), one shaft; 14kts surfaced (15kts submerged).

The postwar Italian Navy's first submarines were three World War II boats, two *Flutto* and one *Acciaio* class, that were eventually rebuilt with streamlined bows and conning towers, and given new equipment. Five modernised *Gato* and *Balao* class submarines were transferred from America, but the first to be built in Italy after World War II were the *Enrico Toti* class. As requirements changed, their design was recast several times, but was finalised before construction began as a coastal hunter-killer submarine. Intended for the shallow and confined waters of the central Mediterranean and Adriatic, their restricted surface range is no handicap, and enables the size to be kept down. They are small and highly manoeuvrable, with a teardrop hull and single screw, and they have diesel-electric drive. The active sonar is mounted in a dome on top of the bow, and the passive sonar is contained in the stern. The four torpedo tubes are also mounted in the bow. They have been succeeded in production by the much larger *Nazario Sauro* class, the first of which was launched on 9 October 1976. To maintain the size of Italy's submarine force, two more modernised *Balaos* and two *Tang* class submarines were transferred from America between 1972 and 1974.

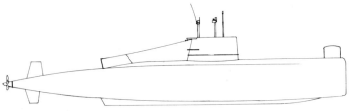

Above: The *Toti* class has a very clean teardrop hull with a single screw. Submerged speed is 15 knots.

Left: *Lazzaro Mocenigo* (S-514) of the *Toti* class. The dome on the bow houses active sonar; passive set is underneath in the stem.

Right: These coastal hunter-killer submarines have four 21in (533mm) torpedo tubes and are designed for Mediterranean operations.

Sparviero Class

Guided missile hydrofoils

Seven ships including *Sparviero* (P-420).

Country of origin: Italy.
Displacement: 62·5 tons full load.
Dimensions: *Hull:* length overall 75·3ft (23m); beam 22·9ft (7m); draught 4·3ft (1·3m). *Foils down:* length overall 80·7ft (24·6m); beam 39·7ft (12·1m); draught hullborne 14·4ft (4·4m); draught foilborne 4·3ft (1·3m).
Armament: Two Otomat 2 SSMs in single launchers; one 3in (76mm) gun in single mounting
Propulsion: One Rolls Royce Proteus gas turbine driving water-jet, 4500bhp; one diesel; maximum speed 52kts.

In the early 1960s the Americans built three experimental hydrofoil patrol boats. These were tested for several years, then between 1966 and 1968 two competitive patrol hydrofoils were built. *Flagstaff* (PGH-1), built by Grumman, was a conventional surface piercing hydrofoil with two struts forward and one aft. *Tucumcari* (PGH-2), based on the previous *High Point* (PCH-1), adopted her fully submerged foil system. This uses one strut forward and two aft. It is inherently unstable, and when foil-borne relies on a small computer and a wave height sensing system to keep the foils submerged and hull clear of the water. The foils can be retracted for cruising. *Tucumcari* (PGH-2) displaced 58 tons (59 tonnes) light, and was armed at one time with one 40mm and two twin 0·5in (12·7mm) machine-guns and one 81mm mortar. Powered by one Rolls Royce Proteus gas turbine with water-jets when foil-borne, and a General Motors diesel for cruising, she had a foil-borne speed of over 40kts. She was discarded in 1973, but in her five years of trials operated successfully in Sea State 6, despite being designed for Sea State 4. *Sparviero* (P-420) is an improved version of *Tucumcari*

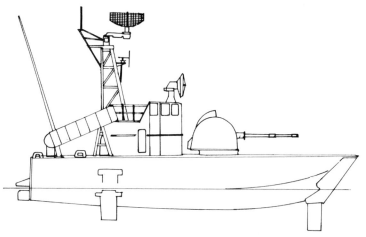

Above: *Sparviero* class. Note the extended foils and 76mm gun.

with a slightly larger hull and greatly improved armament. She was designed and bult by Alinavi, a consortium of Boeing, the Italian government and the Italian commercial hydrofoil builder Carlo Rodriguez. She was intended as the basis for a NATO hydrofoil, but nine of this class were authorised for the Italian Navy in the 1975 *Legge Navale*. She is well suited for short-range operations in the Mediterranean, and has successfully fired Otomat Mk1 SSM, which have an effective range of over 37 miles (31nm). Four hydrofoils are in commission and the remaining three will join the fleet in late 1980/early 1981.

Below: *Sparviero*. Note the launch tubes for the Otomat ASMs.

Chikugo Class

Frigates
11 ships including *Chikugo* (DE-215); *Teshio* (DE-222).

Country of origin: Japan
Displacement: 1470-1500 tons (1700–1730 full load).
Dimensions: Length overall 305.5ft (93.1m); beam 35.5ft (10.8m); draught 11.5ft (3.5m).
Armament: Two 3in (76mm) guns in twin mounting, two 40mm AA guns in twin mounting; one ASROC Mk16 octuple launcher; two triple Mk32 torpedo tubes.
Propulsion: Four diesels (16,000shp), twin shafts; 25kts.

The first Japanese postwar frigates were Japanese and American World War II destroyer escorts. Both steam and diesel propulsion were tried in the

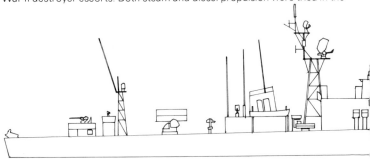

Haruna Class

Helicopter destroyers
Two ships: *Haruna* (DD 141); *Hiei* (DD 142).

Country of origin: Japan.
Displacement: 4700 tons.
Dimensions: Length overall 502ft (153m); beam 57.4ft (17.5m); draught 16.7ft (5.1m).
Aircraft: Three Sikorsky H-SS2 helicopters.
Armament: Two 5in (127mm) guns in single mounts; ASROC octuple Mk16 launcher; two triple US Mk32 torpedo tubes.
Propulsion: Two geared turbines (70,000shp), twin shafts; 32kts.

The Japanese Maritime Self Defence Force is limited to a purely defensive function, and as a result it has not been permitted to build any major warship that might be used in an offensive role. Therefore, unlike other helicopter

Left: *Haruna* fires an ASROC anti-submarine missile. Designed for a purely defensive role, she has a heavy anti-submarine armament.

1953 programme escorts, but steam power was abandoned in the subsequent *Isuzu* class, built between 1960 and 1964. These were flush decked diesel powered frigates of 1,490 tons (1,510 tonnes) standard displacement armed with a twin 3in (76mm) mount fore and aft. The first pair have a single Weapon Able A/S rocket-launcher in B position, with a four-barrel 12in (305mm) rocket-launcher, while the second pair have a triple-barrel Bofors 14·75in (375mm) A/S rocket-launcher and six A/S torpedo tubes. They have hull-mounted sonar, with VDS in two ships. The *Chikugo* class were developed from the *Isuzus*, but have an ASROC A/S launcher and bow and variable depth sonar. They have a much larger bridge, and the ASROC launcher is mounted just aft of the funnel. Their twin 3in (76mm) mount is forward of the bridge and the twin 40mm mount is at the stern, just forward of the variable depth sonar. The later members of the class incorporated minor improvements. A larger version, the *Yamagumo/Minegumo* class destroyers, built since 1964, have a standard displacement of 2150 tons (2184 tonnes) and a speed of 27kts. They have a very similar armament to the *Isuzus* and *Chikugos*, but the second group had a landing pad and hangar for DASH helicopters, which were replaced by ASROC in 1977. The frigates are too small to carry a helicopter and a balanced anti-aircraft and anti-submarine armament, but like all postwar Japanese warships they operate within range of land-based anti-submarine aircraft.

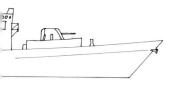

Left: *Chikugo*. The eleven frigates of the Chikugo class are the smallest warships in the world to mount ASROC. Like all other Japanese Maritime Defence Force ships they are designed to fight under shore-based air cover and thus have light air defence systems.

equipped destroyers and cruisers. the *Haruna* class have been optimised for the anti-submarine role, with a very limited anti-aircraft and surface capability. This has, however, meant that the *Harunas* carry virtually the same anti-submarine armament as the Italian *Andrea Doria* helicopter cruisers on 1,300 tons (1,320 tonnes) less standard displacement. *Haruna* carries her two 5in (127mm) Mk 42 guns in single mounts, forward, with the ASROC launcher between B gun and the massive bridge. The uptakes are arranged in a mack which is surmounted by a lattice mast. The hangar, which can accommodate three HHS-2 helicopters, is an integral part of the superstructure. The flight deck stretches the entire aft third of the ship. The Mk 32 torpedo tubes are in two triple mounts one on either side of the bridge. The armament and much of the equipment is American, as with all postwar Japanese ships. Two improved *Harunas*, the *Shirane* class, have been built. These go far towards remedying the *Harunas'* deficiencies in anti-aircraft armament, having a BPDM Sea Sparrow SAM launcher and two twin 35mm anti-aircraft guns in addition to the *Haruna's* armament. They are slightly larger, having a standard displacement of 5,200 tons (5,280 tonnes).

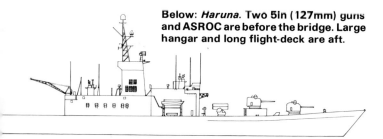

Below: *Haruna*. Two 5in (127mm) guns and ASROC are before the bridge. Large hangar and long flight-deck are aft.

Aist Class

Air cushion vehicles
Eight craft.

Country of origin: Soviet Union
Displacement: 220 tons.
Dimensions: length overall 150ft (45.7m); beam 60ft (18.3m).
Armament: Two twin 30mm cannon.
Propulsion: Two gas turbines driving four propellers and four lift fans; 70kts.

The Soviet Union, and especially the Navy, has shown itself remarkably eager to seize upon and develop new ideas in marked contrast to the normal conservatism of the Russian character. They have, therefore, been in the

forefront of development of the ACV and there are many such craft in civil use, while the navy currently has 52 in commission, 18 with the Baltic Fleet, 18 with the Pacific Fleet and 16 shared between the Black and Caspian Seas.

Eleven 15-ton *Lebed* class have been in service since 1967 and these small craft paved the way for the 27-ton *Gus* class, which is designed to carry 50 Soviet marines on amphibious operations. These ACVs are powered by three 780hp gas turbines; two for propulsion and one for lift, and are a navalised version of the civil *Skate* class. Next to appear was the impressive *Aist* class, which is specifically designed for naval use. Eight are known to be in service, but more will undoubtedly appear, adding significantly to the Soviet capability to carry out rapid, short-range coastal strikes against NATO targets in Scandinavia and on the Baltic.

Below: Nowhere has the British invention of the hovercraft been seized upon more eagerly than in the USSR. This *Aist* class has been developed specifically for use by the Naval Infantry.

Below: This *Gus* class ACV is a naval version of the 50-seat *Skate* class.

Charlie Class

Nuclear submarines
Charlie I class: 12 boats; *Charlie II* class: 3+ boats.

Country of origin: Soviet Union
Displacement: *I*—3900 tons surfaced (4700 tons submerged); *II*—4300 tons surfaced (5200 tons submerged).
Dimensions: *I*—Length overall 308ft (93.9m); beam 32.5ft (9.9m); draught 24.6ft (7.5m). *II*—Length overall 337.5ft (102.9m); beam 32.5ft (9.9m); draught 25.6ft (7.8m).
Armament: Eight SS-N-7 cruise missiles; six 32in (533mm) torpedo tubes (*Charlie I*) or eight 21in (533mm) torpedo tubes (*Charlie II*).
Propulsion: One nuclear reactor, two steam turbines (30,000shp), one shaft; 17kts surfaced, 27kts submerged (*Charlie I*); 20kts. surfaced, 33kts submerged (*Charlie II*).

The shortcomings of the *Echo* class were readily apparent to the Soviet Navy and the next class of nuclear cruiser-missile submarines largely rectified these faults. Although the *Charlies* are still noisier than foreign nuclear submarines, they are a great improvement on the *Echos*. They have much the same hull form and machinery as the *Victor I* class nuclear torpedo-armed submarines, and have a similarly high submerged speed. They are fitted with eight tubes on the bow casing for SSN-7 SSM cruise-missiles. These have a range of about 30 miles (25nm), and so do not require mid-course guidance from another ship or aircraft, and they can be launched submerged, thus greatly decreasing the chances of detection. The *Charlie II* class is an enlarged version with improved capabilities and one similar but slightly longer cruise-missile submarine, the *Papa* class, has also been seen. However, even the *Charlie IIs* are not so sophisticated as the US nuclear submarines, which can launch Harpoon anti-ship missiles from standard torpedo tubes. This missile is much smaller and less vulnerable than its Russian counterparts, and the US submarines may soon be fitted with

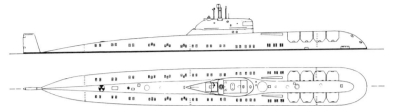

Above: *Charlie I* class nuclear-powered cruise missile submarine.

Above: A *Charlie I* nuclear cruise-missile submarine. These 4,700-ton boats mount eight SSN-7 SSMs and have eight 21in (533mm) torpedo tubes. Submerged speed is about 27 knots.

submarine-launched long-range cruise-missiles which are ejected from standard torpedo tubes submerged. The Soviet Navy has not yet developed an equivalent weapon system.

Below: With the *Charlie* class Soviet naval designers have at last paid attention to reducing underwater noise and the hull form is a great improvement on classes like the *Echo II* (q.v.). Even so, Soviet boats are still noisier than those in the West.

Delta I, II and III Class

Nuclear ballistic missile submarines

Delta I class: 19 boats; *Delta II* class: 5 boats; *Delta III* class: 7+ boats.

Country of origin: Soviet Union
Displacement: *I*—8350 tons surfaced (9300 tons submerged); *II*, *III*—9350 tons surfaced (11,750 tons submerged).
Dimensions: *I*—Length overall 446·1ft (136m), beam 38ft (11·6m), draught 32·8ft (10m). *II*, *III*—Length overall 498·6ft (152.7m); beam 38·7ft (11·8m); draught 35·5ft (10·2m).
Armament: *I*—Twelve SS-N-8 SLBMs, *II*—Sixteen SS-N-8 SLBMs, *III*—Sixteen SS-N-18 SLBMs; all—Six 21in (533mm) torpedo tubes.
Propulsion: One nuclear reactor, two steam turbine (60,000shp), twin shafts; 22kts surfaced, 30 knots submerged (28kts submerged for *Delta II* and *Delta III*).

Up to 1973 the Americans had a considerable advantage in the quality of their SLBMs, but in that year the Russians introduced the SSN-8 SLBM. With a range of over 4,000 miles (3,500nm) and a CEP of only 1,300ft (400m), this not only has a larger range than the Poseidon but also outranges Trident. Initial trials were made using a *Hotel III* class nuclear ballistic missile submarine, and the missile is fitted in the *Delta I* and *II* class submarines. The *Delta I* class carries 12 missiles in two rows of six abaft the

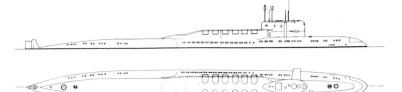

Above: *Delta I* class, nuclear-powered ballistic missile submarine.

fin, and the considerably enlarged *Delta IIs* carry two more rows of two missiles. The SS-N-8 Mod 1 carries a single warhead of between 1 and 2 megatons, the Mod 2 has three MRNs and the Mod 3 has been tested with three MIRVs. A second slipway was built at the Severodvinsk shipyard in 1975 to enable the class to be built more quickly. The *Delta III* is similar in size and other details to the *Delta II*, but carries sixteen SS-N-18 missiles, which have a range of some 5000 miles and MIRVed warheads. These submarines are a great threat to the USA, because they can hit targets in the United States from launching areas in the Western Pacific or Murmansk regions, well out of reach of any known countermeasures.

Below: A *Delta II* class submarine. This boat is based on the *Yankee* hull (q.v.) but because the SSN-8 missile is longer than the SSN-6 an even larger box-like covering is required abaft the fin.

Echo II Class

Nuclear submarines
29 boats.

Country of origin: Soviet Union
Displacement: 4800 tons surfaced (5800 tons submerged).
Dimensions: Length overall 384·7ft (117.3m); beam 30.2ft (9.2m);
draught 25·5ft (7·9m).
Armament: Eight tubes for SS-N-3 cruise missiles, but 20 boats have been
modified to take SS-N-12.
Propulsion: One nuclear reactor, two steam turbines (30,000shp), twin
shafts; 20kts surfaced, 25kts submerged.

With the introduction in 1948 of the North American AJ Savage, the
American carrier forces had an aircraft capable of carrying an atomic bomb.
For the first time the American carrier forces represented a major threat to
the Soviet Union. In the 1950s the Russians developed a number of cruise-
missiles, one of which, the SSN-3 was intended for use in submarines. This
could be launched at a long distance from the carrier task force's defences
and at the time represented a credible answer to the threat posed by that
task force. The first submarines to be equipped with the SSN-3 were the
Whisky twin cylinder and the *Whisky long bin* conversions, but these were
very crude, and the first true cruise-missile armed submarines were the five
boats of the *Echo I* class, built between 1958 and 1962. Nuclear-powered,
these were very similar to the *November* nuclear torpedo-armed and *Hotel*
nuclear ballistic missile submarines. The *Echo Is* carried six SSN-3 'Shaddock'
turbo-jet powered SSMs in individual elevating tubes in the casing, two
ahead and four abaft the fin. These surface-launched missiles have a range of
about 475 miles (400nm) and can carry either a high explosive or nuclear
warhead, but require mid-course guidance. This makes both the missile and
the aircraft or ship giving that guidance vulnerable to countermeasures. The
Echo I class were all converted between 1973 and 1974. The SSN-3
launchers were removed and they are now armed solely with torpedoes.
The *Echo I* class were soon superseded by the *Echo IIs,* which differ mainly

**Below: An *Echo II* class submarine. 29 of these nuclear-powered
boats are in service with the Pacific and Northern fleets.**

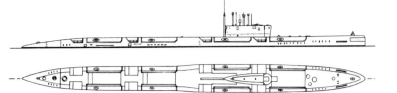

Above: *Echo II* class entered service in 1963; 8 SSN-12 are carried.

by having a slightly lengthened hull incorporating another pair of SSN-3 launchers abaft the fin. Some twenty *Echo II*s have been fitted with SS-N12 cruise missiles to replace the SS-N-3.

The *Echo II*s are still a useful design and are deployed with the Pacific and Northern Fleets, with a few detached to the Mediterranean. The *Echos* are even noisier than the *Novembers*, because of the large holes in the casing around each missile launcher. This, combined with the need to surface to launch the missiles, makes them relatively easy to detect.

Below: A damaged *Echo II* submarine limping home to the USSR. These boats carry 8 SSN-12 anti-ship cruise missiles, although some still carry the older SSN-3. The large wells around each missile tube make this submarine very noisy and easy to detect.

Grisha Class

Corvettes

Grisha I class: 15+ ships. *Grisha II* class: 6+ ships.
Grisha III class: 14+ ships.

Country of origin: Soviet Union
Displacement: 900 tons (1000 full load).
Dimensions: Length overall 236.2ft (72m); beam 32.8ft (10m), draught 11ft (3.6m).
Armament: One twin SA-N-4 SAM launcher (*Grisha I* and *III*); one twin 57mm gun mount (*Grisha I* and *III*) or two twin 57m gun mounts (*Grisha II*), Gatling gun (*Grisha III*); two twin 21in (533mm) torpedo tubes; two 12-barrel MBU launchers.
Propulsion: One gas turbine (12,000shp); two diesels (18,000shp); three shafts; 30kts.

Since World War II the Russians have progressively developed designs of coastal anti-submarine vessels. The first postwar-type, the *Kronstadt* class, was based on prewar submarine catcher designs. They were diesel-powered vessels of 310 tons (315 tonnes) standard displacement. The next class, the *So 1s*, introduced the MBU anti-submarine rocket. These displaced 215 tons (218 tonnes) light. The *Potr* class, built between 1961 and 1968, carried a much heavier anti-submarine armament and had mixed diesel and gas turbine machinery in a much larger hull which had a standard displacement of 550 tons (560 tonnes). They mounted two 12-barrel MBU-2500 rocket-launchers and two 16in (406mm) anti-submarine torpedo tubes as well as a twin 57mm gun turret. The *Grisha I* and *II* classes are

Right: There are three variants of the *Grisha* class. *Grisha I* has a twin SAN-4 launcher on the fo'csle and one twin 57mm turret on the quarterdeck. On *Grisha II* the SAN-4 launcher is replaced by a second twin 57mm turret. *Grisha III* reverts to the same armament as *Grisha I*, but with an additional Gatling mount aft and changes in the radar fit. According to some reports the *Grisha II* was developed for the KGB maritime patrols for use in border areas.

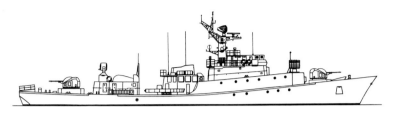

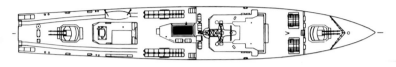

Above: *Grisha II* with twin 57mm mount for'd in place of SAN-4.

enlarged versions of the *Potrs*, with the hull again enlarged to improve seaworthiness and to enable a heavier anti-aircraft amament to be mounted. The *Grisha I* class mounts a retractable twin SAN-4 SAM launcher forward, which is replaced in the *Grisha IIs* by a second twin 57mm gun turret. In order to accommodate a balanced armament; the *Grishas* have been enlarged into something that is no longer a small expendable vessel, but a fully fledged warship capable of defending itself adequately against aircraft whilst possessing a reasonable anti-submarine armament. Examples of both the *Grisha I* and *Grisha II* are to be found in all the Russian fleets. *Grisha III* has a different radar fit, plus a new Gatling turret mounted aft.

Ivan Rogov Class

Landing platform docks
Two ships

Country of origin: Soviet Union
Displacement: 11,000 tons (13,100 full load).
Dimensions: Length overall 521.6ft (159m); beam 80.2ft (24.5m); draught 21.2ft (6.5m).
Armament: One twin SA-N-4 SAM launcher; one twin 76mm gun mounting; four 23mm Gatlings; one BM-21 (naval) rocket launcher.
Propulsion: Four diesels; 20,000shp; 20kts.

One of the most remarkable expansions in capability by the Soviet Navy has been in amphibious warfare, but, because landing ships lack the glamour of destroyers or cruisers, this has passed largely unnoticed in the West.

The first major class was the *Polnochniy* landing craft tank (LCT) of which some 60 have been built. There are four groups within the class varying in full load displacement from 950-1250 tons. They have a carrying capacity of six tanks. A further 23 *Polnochniys* have been built at Gdansk for the Polish Navy.

Next to appear were the 14 landing ships tank (LST) of the *Alligator* class, with a full load displacement of 4500 tons. Commissioned in the late 'sixties these ships serve regularly in African and Asian water, usually with Soviet marines embarked, and they represent a major extension of Soviet political and military power.

In a new departure the Soviet Navy then ordered *Rapucha* class LSTs from Poland, thus, of course, releasing space in Soviet dockyards for other warship construction. The first was commissioned in 1975 and they have appeared at a rate of three per year since. The *Rapuchas* have a displacement of 4400 tons full load and have greater personnel accommodation than the *Alligators*. The East German navy has built 10 LSTs of the *Frösch* class, which are similar, but not identical, to the Polish *Rapuchas*.

In 1978 the *Ivan Rogov* appeared; this is a 13,000 ton LPD of a novel and sensible design. It is quite clearly intended to project Soviet power to the farthest parts of the world, and has a capacity for a battalion of Soviet

marines, some 40 tanks, and other supporting vehicles. It has bow and stern doors, and is capable of accommodating both Air Cushion Vehicles (ACVs) and helicopters.

The Soviet Navy, and certain of its Warsaw Pact allies, is assembling an amphibious force with great strategic potential, and the West should take careful note of it.

Above: An overhead view of the *Ivan Rogov* showing the very large helicopter landing areas and the staggered funnels. This ship can carry a marine battalion, 40 tanks and support vehicles.

Below: *Ivan Rogov* appeared in 1978 and is a novel design of LPD.

Kashin Class

Destroyers
Six modified ships.

Country of origin: Soviet Union
Displacement: 3750 tons (4500 full load).
Dimensions: Length overall 470ft (143·3m); beam 52·5ft (15·9m); draught 15·4ft (4·7m).
Armament: Four SA-N-1 SAM launchers; two twin 3in (76mm) guns; two 12-barrelled MBU, two 6-barrelled MBU A/S launchers; one quin 21in (533mm) torpedo tubes.
Propulsion: Four sets gas turbines, 96,000hp; twin shafts; 35kts.

The early part of the post-War expansion of the Soviet Navy was based on producing a large fleet of destroyers. The *Skory* class was succeeded by the *Kotlins* (built 1954-57), the *Kildins* (1958) *SAM Kotlins* (1964-72), and *Kanins* (1968-77). Western navies became progressively more impressed as each new class appeared, although there was nothing to be especially apprehensive about since they were all strictly conventional and most of their design features could be attributed to German or Italian influence.

Any complacency which remained, however, was rudely shattered when the first *Kashin* appeared in 1963. Their rakish lines match the innovations in the design: the first major warship to rely solely on gas turbines for propulsion, and the first ship to rely so heavily on missiles.

The other major surprise for the West was the remarkable collection of electronic devices on the ship. The mounting of antennas and electronic equipment on board a warship is difficult if mutual interference is to be avoided, but the Soviets seem to have found an effective answer.

The *Kashins* started an updating programme in 1974, six modified ships having been identified so far. This consists of adding an extra 10ft (3.05m) to the hull and mounting four SS-N-2 SSM launchers, four Gatling-type close range defence weapons, and a variable depth sonar. A raised helicopter platform is built on the stern. The electronic fit has also been altered and improved.

Surprisingly, the *Kashins* seem to be the last of the destroyer line in the Soviet Navy, with attention now being concentrating on larger and more heavily armed cruisers in the 6000-9000 ton class.

Above: *Strogiy,* one of the unmodified *Kashin* class destroyers of the Soviet Navy. This class first appeared in 1963 and caused considerable surprise in the West for their many daring innovations. They were the first major ships to rely solely on gas-turbines and the first to place such reliance on missiles.

Below: Another unmodified *Kashin* class destroyer. The modifications comprise lengthening the hull by 10ft (3.05m), mounting four launchers for SSN-2 (modified) SSMs, building a new stern helicopter platform and installing variable depth sonar and four Gatling guns. Only six are known to have been converted.

Kiev Class

Anti-submarine cruisers/aircraft carriers

Two ships: *Kiev; Minsk;* and two building: *Kharkov* (?) and *Novorossiisk* (?).

Country of origin: Soviet Union
Displacement: 32,000 tons (38,000 full load).
Dimensions: Length overall 898·7ft (274m); beam overall 157·4ft (48m); draught 27·2ft (8·3m).
Aircraft: 12 Forger A, 1 Forger B, 30 Hormone helicopters.
Armament: Four twin SS-N-12 SSM launchers, two twin SA-N-3 SAM launchers, one twin SUW-N-1 A/S launcher; two twin 76mm gun mountings, eight 30mm Gatling guns; ten 21in (533mm) torpedo tubes have only been seen on *Kiev* but may have been removed; two 12-barrel MBU 2500A A/S launchers.
Propulsion: Four steam turbines (160,000shp), four shafts; 32kts.

Although there had been considerable interest in both airships and fixed-wing aircraft in both the Imperial and Soviet Navies, all plans to build any form of aircraft-carrier failed to materialise. These varied from a cruiser *(Komintern)* conversion to seaplane carrier, through two custom-designed seaplane carriers for the Pacific, to two fixed-wing carriers in the Third Five year plan (1938-1942). The first was abandoned and the remainder cancelled. During and after World War II a formidable naval air force was built up, consisting of some 4,000 fighters, bombers and reconnaissance planes. In the Khruschev reorganisation this was drastically cut back and its fighters removed, but at no time was there any move back to planning aircraft-carriers. In fact the arguments for and against such ships were conducted with considerable heat and vigour. The first *Kresta I* cruiser, commissioned in early 1967, carried a helicopter with a hangar and paved the way for the appearance a year later of *Moskva*, an 18,000 ton (18,288 tonne) helicopter-carrier with 18 'Hormone' helicopters embarked. She and

**Below: The excellent lines and heavy armament of the *Kiev* class illustrate the skill and ingenuity of Soviet naval designers.
It is clear from the plan view how the deck has been divided into distinct parts; flight-deck, superstructure, weapons area.**

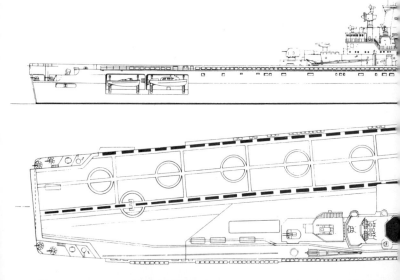

Above: *Kiev* at sea off the British Isles on her first cruise.

her sister *Leningrad* may well have been planned as the forerunners of a large class but no more were completed. Their duties were clearly anti-submarine as reflected in the majority of Soviet type designations for their major ships. They did, however, have considerable potential in other directions such as intervention situations. Shortly before *Moskva* commissioned the first Soviet V/STOL aircraft appeared at an air display near Moscow. Subsequently little else was seen of this type of aircraft and when a large hull was seen building at Nikolayev in 1971 it was no great strain on the intelligence to marry up the two. The first British Harrier had flown in 1966 and in the next five years had carried out a series of deck-landings on the ships of several navies. When *Kiev* finally emerged from the Black Sea in August 1976 something totally new was revealed. Not only was she an aircraft-carrier in all but name, although restricted to the operation of V/STOL aircraft and helicopters, she was also a very heavily armed warship. ▶

Overleaf: Lined up on the flight-deck of *Kiev* are four Kamov Ka-25 (NATO designation: Hormone B) anti-submarine helicopters. In the parking area is a Yakovlev Yak-36 (NATO designation: Forger A) VTOL attack aircraft.

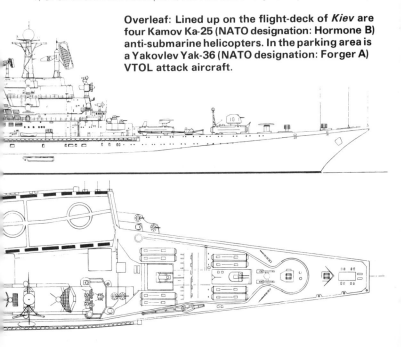

Above: Twelve of *Kiev's* **normal complement of 30 Ka-25 (Hormone) helicopters are on deck, eight of them with folded rotor blades. Note the SAM launcher and 76mm turret at after end of island.**

Below right: The second *Kiev* **class carrier,** *Minsk,* **is refuelled at sea by the** *Berezhina,* **the first of a new type of fleet replenishment ship. Also being replenished is a** *Kara II* **cruiser.**

Eight surface-to-surface launchers decorated her fo'c's'le, and missiles of other kinds dotted her upper deck; 76mm (3in) guns and Gatlings provided more conventional armament. New radars had been fitted and she carried sonar—an enormous departure from US practice where neither sonar nor guns are fitted in carriers and the only missiles are for point-defence. The somewhat tentative approach of the V/STOL pilots and general Soviet inexperience in this field, particularly when compared to the highly professional US Navy approach, may have been behind part of this design. Nevertheless *Kiev* is a very potent warship capable of operating to advantage in both war and intervention situations. She may suffer from her comparatively low freeboard but her successors will no doubt benefit from lessons learned—flat-faced sponsons at the head of the flight deck as an example. The next generation may well be larger and it is certain that the embarkation of ordinary fixed-wing aircraft, including the many problems of catapults, arrester-wires, landing-aids and training, have been examined. The second ship of this class, *Minsk,* transitted the Turkish Straits on 25 February 1979, and two more are known to be under construction.

Above: Down the centreline of *Kiev's* foredeck are two 12-barrel MBU 2500 AS rocket-launchers, one twin SAN-3 SAM launcher, a twin 76mm gun turret and a second twin SAN-3 launcher. These are flanked by eight SSN-12 ASM launchers.

Kresta I and II Class and Kara Class

Guided missile cruisers

20+ ships: *Kresta 1 class* (4 ships): *Vice-Admiral Drozd; Admiral Zozulya; Sevastopol; Vladivostok; Kresta II class* (11 ships) including *Admiral Isakov; Marshal Voroshilov. Kara class* (5+ ships): including *Nikolayev; Azov.*

Kresta I and II class:
Country of origin: Soviet Union
Displacement: *I*–6140 tons (7500 full load), *II*–6000 tons (7600 full load).
Dimensions: Length overall— *1* — 510ft (155.5m), *II* — 519.9ft (158.5m); beam (both) 55.7ft (17m); draught (both) 19.7ft (6m).
Aircraft: One Hormone helicopter.
Armament: *I*—Two twin SS-N-3 SSM launchers, two twin SA-N-1 SAM launchers; two twin 57mm guns, four 23mm Gatling guns (*Drozd* only); two quin torpedo tubes. *II*— Two quad SS-N-14 ASM launchers, two twin SA-N-3 SAM launchers; two twin 57mm guns, four 30mm Gatling guns; two 12-barrel MBV launchers.
Propulsion: Steam turbines (100,000shp), twin shafts; 35kts. (*Kresta II* 34kts).

Kara class:
Country of origin: Soviet Union
Displacement: 8200 tons (9500 full load).
Dimensions: Length overall 570ft (173.8m); beam 60ft (18.3m); draught 20ft (6.2m).
Aircraft: One Hormone helicopter.
Armament: Two quad SS-N-14 ASM launchers, twin SA-N-3 SAM launcher, two twin SA-N-4 SAM launchers; two twin 76mm gun mounts, four 23mm Gatling guns; two quin 21in torpedo tubes; two 12-barrel and two 6-barrel MBV launchers.
Propulsion: Four gas turbines (120,000shp), twin shafts; 32kts.

The Russian guided-missile cruisers were originally built in response to the threat posed to the Soviet Union by the large American carrier force. The four *Kynda* class were the first Russian cruisers to be designed for this purpose. Built between 1960 and 1965, with a standard displacement of 4,800 tons (4,877 tonnes), they were armed with two quadruple-launchers for SSN-3 'Shaddock' SSMs. The large cruise missile has a range of about 475 miles (400nm) and is also mounted in the early Russian cruise-missile armed submarines. The *Kyndas* have a SAN-1 'Goa' SAM twin-launcher ▶

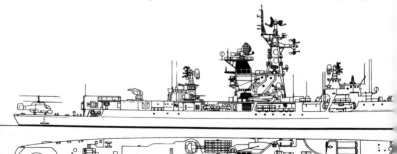

Above: A *Kresta II* guided-missile cruiser photographed while shadowing the NATO 'Exercise Ocean Safari 1975'. Shown to advantage are the folding-roofed hangar for the Ka-25 (Hormone A) holicopter and the very small landing platform. Powered by two steam turbines, *Kresta IIs* have a maximum speed of 34 knots

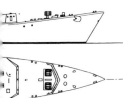

Left: The *Kresta II* is an enlarged version of the *Kynda* class, with a very powerful anti-aircraft and anti-submarine armament. *Kresta I* was the first Soviet class to have permanent facilities for a helicopter (Hormone A), which is required for target location and mid-course guidance for the SSN-3 (Shaddock) missile.

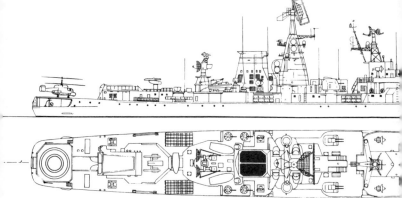

Above: *Kara* **class cruiser. These are enlarged versions of the**
Kresta **class with improved weapons and electronics fits, and**
gas-turbine engines. Note the large mast and the very large,
separate funnel, as well as the profusion of radomes and antennas.

forward and two twin 3in (76mm) mounts aft. Two tracking radars are fitted
for the SSMs, enabling them to engage two targets simultaneously, but no
helicopter is carried. This makes the *Kyndas* dependent on other ships or
aircraft for mid-course guidance for the SSMs. The *Kresta Is* are enlarged
developments of the *Kyndas*. Whereas the latter design gave priority to the
SSM armament, the *Kresta Is* (and the *Kresta II* and *Kara* classes developed
from them) have a very powerful anti-aircraft and anti-submarine armament.
In the *Kresta Is* the SSN-3 SSMs are mounted in pairs on either side of the
bridge. They are double-ended ships, with a SAN-1 'Goa' SAM twin-launcher
fore and aft on deckhouse magazines. Whereas the *Kyndas* have two
prominent masts and funnels, the *Kresta Is* have their SSM guidance radar
on a single enormous mack amidships. Instead of the *Kyndas'* long
quarterdeck, the *Kresta Is* have a very short one with a helicopter pad and
hangar mounted on it. The Kamov Ka-25 'Hormone' was designed for anti-
submarine work, but could also be used for mid-course guidance for the
SSMs. By the late 1960s the A/S problem apparently took precedence and
the *Kresta IIs* were fitted with two quadruple launchers for the long-range
SSN-14 A/S weapon. The SAN-1 'Goa' SAMs are replaced by the improved
longer ranged SAN-3 'Goblet' SAMs. Close-in anti-aircraft defence is
provided by the 30mm mounts amidships. Bow sonar is fitted, and as with all
modern Soviet warships, a powerful anti-submarine armament is fitted. The
helicopter pad and hangar are raised by one deck, which makes them less
likely to be damaged in rough seas, and this and the large 'Topsail' 3-dimen-
sional radar serve to distinguish the *Kresta IIs* from the *Kresta Is*. The *Karas*
are enlarged gas-turbine powered versions of the *Kresta IIs*. The extra size
has been used to mount two retractable SAN-4 SAM twin-launchers, and the
heavy anti-aircraft armament has been increased in calibre. They are the first
large warships to have gas turbines, which have been in service with the
Soviet Navy in the *Kashin* class destroyers for over a decade. The *Karas* can
be distinguished from the *Kresta IIs* by their longer hull and the large
separate funnel necessitated by the use of gas turbines. Compared with
contemporary American cruisers, the Russian ships are much more heavily
armed, but the long-ranged American ships have large and very seaworthy
hulls, and until recently they have relied mainly on the carrier-borne aircraft
for long-range surface attack. They are intended mainly as anti-submarine
and anti-aircraft escorts, whereas the Russian ships have not only had to
provide protection against the more sophisticated American submarines and
aircraft, but also provide their own long-range surface attack capability. As a
result the Russian ships have a relatively short range.

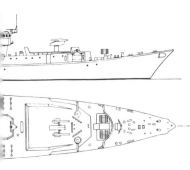

Below: The antenna complexes on *Kara* class cruiser *Ochakov* are clearly shown. The two identical arrays above the bridge and abaft the funnel are 'Headlight groups', which control the SAN-4 SAM missiles. At the rear of the bridge is 'Head Net C', an air surveillance radar, capable of both search and height-finding. Atop the mast is the 'Top Sail' 3-dimensional radar antenna, used for long-range air surveillance and target designation. Integrating these electronic systems is a complex task.

Below: *Kara* class cruiser in the Mediterranean. The two quadruple launch silos for the SSN-14 are prominent on either side of the bridge. Thought at first to be anti-ship missiles, SSN-14 is now assumed to be an anti-submarine weapon system.

Krivak Class

Guided missile frigates

25+ ships: *Krivak I class* (18 ships) including *Bditelny; Bodry.*
Krivak II class (7+ ships).

Country of origin: Soviet Union
Displacement: 3300 tons (3600 full load).
Dimensions: Length overall 404.8ft (123.4m); beam 45.9ft (14m); draught 16.4ft (5m).
Armament: One quad SS-N-14 ASM launcher, two twin SA-N-4 SAM launchers; two twin 3in (76mm) guns (*Krivak I*) or two single 100mm guns *(Krivak II);* two quad 21in (53mm) torpedo tubes; two 12-barrel MBU missile launchers.
Propulsion: Four gas turbines (72,000shp), twin shafts; 32kts.

Krivak class. These powerful anti-submarine vessels are classified as Storozhevoy Korabl, meaning Escort Ship, by the Soviet Navy. Note the SSN-14 twin launchers and the retractable SAN-4 twin launchers forward of the bridge and abaft the funnel.

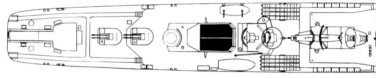

The 19 *Kashin* class guided missile destroyers built between 1962 and 1966 were the world's first operational warships to be fitted with gas turbines. Displacing 3,750 tons (3,810 tonnes) standard, they are a relatively conventional double-ended anti-aircraft design, armed with two SAN-1 'Goa'-SAM twin-launchers. A number of the class have been converted to allow an SSM to be mounted, and to improve the anti-submarine armament. With a 10ft (3m) hull extension, they have four SSN-2 (mod) SSMs, variable depth sonar and a helicopter pad aft. *Otvazkny* of this class was destroyed by an internal explosion in the Black Sea on 31 August 1974. The *Krivaks* take full advantage of the gas turbine's light weight and high power, and mount a very powerful multi-purpose armament on a hull with a very high beam-to-length ratio. Contrary to initial reports these ships are anti-submarine vessels, with a quadruple SSN-14 ASW missile mounting in the bow. The SAN-4 SAM retractable launchers are mounted fore and aft, and the 3in (76mm) twin turrets are mounted aft just ahead of the variable depth sonar. The two quadruple A/S torpedo tubes are fitted either side of the superstructure amidships. These ships have high speed and very heavy armament compared with Western designs, but are not able to operate a helicopter. They must have very cramped accommodation for the necessary electronics and large crew. Unlike most western vessels, their gas turbines are all the same size. Construction continues at about three ships per year.

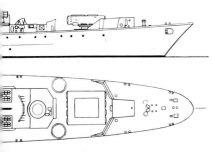

Below: A Soviet Navy *Krivak* class guided-missile frigate photographed in the Baltic. Entering service in 1971 these gas-turbine powered ships mount a powerful A/S armament. There are two sonars: one fixed in the bow, and a Variable Depth Sonar (VDS) on the stern. Although very strongly armed compared with Western ships of the same size, range is poor.

Moskva Class

Anti-submarine cruiser/helicopter carriers

Two ships: *Moskva; Leningrad.*

Country of origin: Soviet Union
Displacement: 14,500 tons (18,000 full load).
Dimensions: Length overall 624.8ft (190.5m); beam overall 111.5ft (34m); draught 24.9ft (7.6m).
Aircraft: 18 Hormone A helicopters.
Armament: Two twin SA-N-3 SAM launchers; two twin 57mm guns; one twin SUWN-1 ASW missile launcher, two 12-tube MBU 2500A launchers.
Propulsion: Geared turbines (100,000shp), twin shafts; 30kts.

By the mid-1960s the Soviet Navy had begun to maintain semi-permanent fleets in the North Atlantic and Mediterranean, in much the same way that the Americans have done since the end of World War II. In addition to the anti-aircraft defence provided by individual ships' normal complements of guns and missiles, some of the older SSM-armed guided-missile destroyers have been converted into specialist anti-aircraft escorts. In the same way, although every modern Soviet warship down to patrol boat size has a multiplicity of anti-submarine weapons and detectors, these are insufficient in themselves to counter the threat posed by the very sophisticated Western nuclear submarines. A requirement therefore existed for a specialist large anti-submarine vessel. The resulting single-ended *Moskva* class helicopter carriers resemble the earlier French *Jeanne d'Arc* (R-97) and the later Italian *Vittorio Veneto* (C-550), but are much larger and more sophisticated ships, equipped not only with a sizeable force of helicopters but also with a ▶

Right: *Moskva* class anti-submarine cruiser. Only two of these very useful ships were built.

Below right: *Moskva*, showing the missile launchers on the foredeck, the concentration of radar antennas on the superstructure, and two Hormone helicopters.

Below: A *Moskva* class anti-submarine cruiser. Note the heavy armament of missile launchers and guns in comparison with, for example, *Illustrious.*

Above: A Nimrod AEW aircraft of the RAF flies over the *Moskva*.

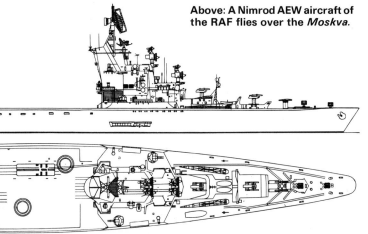

complete range of anti-submarine and anti-aircraft weapons and detectors. They are not intended to operate on their own, and therefore do not require SSMs. The hull design is unique, with the maximum width at flight deck level coming three-quarters aft. There is massive flare to the hull aft to permit a flight deck 295·3ft (90m) long and 115ft (35m) wide to be carried. This has three elevators to the hangar below, two in the flight deck itself and one inside the superstructure at the forward end of the flight deck. The *Moskvas* can operate up to 18 Kamov Ka-25 'Hormone' anti-submarine helicopters with dipping sonars and A/S torpedoes. The quarterdeck is open right aft to allow a variable depth sonar to be operated and they also have a hull mounted sonar. The two MBU-2500 A/S rocket-launchers are mounted in the bows, and immediately behind them there is a SUWN-1 twin-launcher firing FRAS-1 and SSN-14 long-range anti-submarine missiles. Behind this there are two superimposed SAN-3 'Goblet' SAM twin launchers. The two twin 57mm guns are mounted either side of the bridge, and quintuple 21in (533mm) A/S torpedo tubes are fitted either side amidships. The large piled-up superstructure terminates abruptly in a large mack surrounded by 'Topsail' 3-dimensional radar. Despite their unconventional design, the *Moskvas* are good seaboats, able to operate helicopters in rough weather. They are very useful ships, but lack the flexibility of a through-deck design, which is better suited for operating V/STOL aircraft. They have therefore been succeeded by the much larger *Kievs*. *Moskva* was modified for a time to act as a trials ship for the Yakovlev Yak-36 'Forger' V/TOL aircraft.

Below: A US Navy Neptune shadows a *Moskva* class cruiser. Although superficially resembling the earlier French *Jeanne d'Arc*, these ships are, in fact, a purely Soviet concept and provide an excellent balance between functions.

Above: The aircraft lift is down at hangar level in this picture.
18 Hormone ASW helicopters are carried and although tests have
been made with VTOL aircraft it is highly unlikely that they would
be carried operationally.

Nanuchka I, II and III Class

Missile corvettes

Nanuchka I class: 16+ boats; *Nanuchka II* class: 3+ boats; *Nanuchka III* class: 3+ boats.

Country of origin: Soviet Union
Displacement: 800 tons (950 full load).
Dimensions: Length overall 193·5ft (59m); beam 39·6ft (12m); draught 9·9ft (3m).
Armament: *I*—Two triple SS-N-9 SSM launchers, one twin SA-N-4 SAM launcher, one twin 57mm gun. *II*—Two twin SS-N-2 (or SS-N-11) SSM launchers, one twin SA-N-4 SAM launcher; one twin 57mm gun. *III*—Two triple SS-N-9 SSM launchers, one twin SA-N-9 SSM launchers, one twin SA-N-9 SSM launchers, one twin SA-N-4 SAM launcher; one 76mm gun, one Gatling turret.
Propulsion: Six diesels (28,000shp), three shafts; 32kts.

Successors to the *Osas*, the *Nanuchkas* not only carry a much more effective missile, the SSN-9 SSM, but also possess an adequate missile and gun anti-aircraft armament. The large hull also means that the *Nanuchkas* can operate in rough seas, and they have a wide hull to make them steady missile platforms. They complement the anti-submarine *Grisha I* and *II* class corvettes. The SSN-9 missiles have a range of about 68 miles (110km) and require mid-course guidance if fired 'over-the-horizon'. It is of interest to note that the three *Nanuchka IIs* supplied to India are armed with SS-N-2 or 11 missiles and not with SS-N-9. These unusual but very effective ships epitomise the willingness of the Soviet Navy's staff and designers to consider new approaches and to produce revolutionary ships and weapons.

Right: *Nanuchka I* class missile corvette. The ship is dominated by the two triple launchers for the SSN-9 anti-ship missiles.

Below: A *Nanuchka* class corvette anchored astern of a *Kotlin* destroyer, photographed in Kythira anchorage in the Mediterranean.

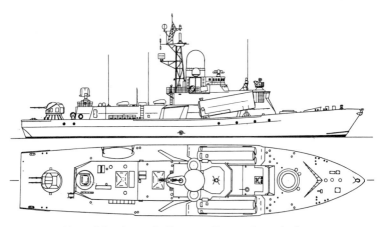

Above: *Nanuchka* class missile corvette, a unique design.

Osa I and II Class

Missile patrol boats
180+ boats.

Country of origin: Soviet Union
Displacement: 160 tons (210 full load).
Dimensions: Length overall 128.7ft (39.3m); beam 25.1ft (7.7m);
draught 5.9ft (1.8m).
Armament: Four SS-N-2 SSM launchers; four 30mm cannon.
Propulsion: Three diesels, 12,000bhp *(Osa I)*; 15,000bhp *(Osa II)*; 36
knots.

The SSN-2 'Styx' SSM is one of several cruise-missiles developed by the
Soviet Union in the mid-1950s, and is specifically intended as an anti-ship
weapon for small surface vessels. It has a range of (?) 27 miles (23nm) and a
high explosive warhead of about 900lbs (400kg). It is mounted on the
Komar and *Osa I* classes. The *Komars*, an adaptation of the *P-6*
torpedo boat design, carry two missiles on their launchers aft. Experience
has shown that larger salvoes are necessary to ensure success and the
Komars are too small to operate in anything other than moderate seas. The
Osa I class, on the other hand, was designed specifically to take 'Styx',
and has four launchers aft on a much larger hull. The *Osa II* class are fitted with
four smaller and lighter launchers for the SSN-2 (an improved 'Styx'), and
was introduced in 1968–1969. A version of the *Osas* without missiles but
possessing a torpedo armament, the *Stenka* class, has been built in
considerable numbers from 1967 onward. The first success obtained by a
shipborne guided missile came on 21 October 1967, when 'Styx' fired from
Egyptian *Komars* sank the Israeli destroyer *Eilat*. Further successes were
obtained by Indian *Osas* during the Indo-Pakistan war of December 1971.
However, these successes were achieved against relatively unsophisticated
targets. The Arab-Israeli war of 1973 showed that these missiles were
obsolete against modern electronic countermeasures. A larger vessel with
better electronics and more sophisticated missiles was needed. This was
realised by the Russians in the late 1960s, and the result was the *Nanuchka*

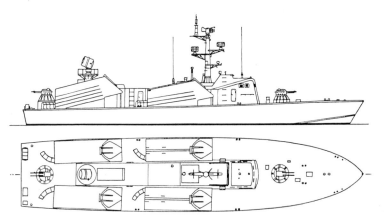

Above: The *Osa* class mounts four SSN-2 'Styx' anti-ship missiles.

Left: *Osa II* dressed overall for inspection. *Osa I* has larger launchers of squarer cross-section for SSN-2 Styx while *Osa II* has smaller, round launchers for SSN-2 (mod) missiles. Note the beamy, hard-chine hull.

Below: An *Osa* class missile patrol boat at sea. This class were quite revolutionary when they first appeared in the early 1950s because they gave small craft the ability to destroy major warships as was proved when the Israeli destroyer *Eilat* was sunk on 21 October 1967. They are now being replaced by hydrofoils.

Sverdlov Class

Cruisers

14 ships including *Sverdlov; Zhdanov.*

Country of origin: Soviet Union
Displacement: 16,000 tons (17,500 full load).
Dimensions: Length overall 689.0ft (210m); beam 72.2ft (22m); draught 24.5ft (7.5m).
Aircraft: Helicopters can be carried only by *Zhdanov* and *Senyavin.*
Armament: Varies greatly between ships. Basic armament is four triple 6in (152mm) gun mountings, plus twelve 3.9in (100mm), sixteen 37mm. Some ships have missiles instead of one or both after 3.9in turrets.
Propulsion: General turbines (110,000shp), twin shafts; 30kts.

In the late 1940s the Russians were very short of modern heavy units, and 24 improved *Chapaevs* were projected. The *Sverdlovs* are very similar to the *Chapaevs*, but have the fo'c's'le break abaft X turret instead of abaft the fore funnel, and they also have a beamier hull, with an improved anti-aircraft and higher powered engines. They are the last all-gun-armed cruisers to be built, and they compare unfavourably in protection and armament with the somewhat earlier American *Oregon City* class, which are of similar size. Nevertheless, they are powerful ships, with a good range and a large anti-aircraft armament. Seventeen were laid down, but only 14 completed before

Below: *Sverdlov* in the English Channel, 1974.

Below: *Sverdlov* class. Armament: 12 6in (152mm) guns in four triple turrets, 12 3.9in (100mm), 16 37mm, but some vary from this.

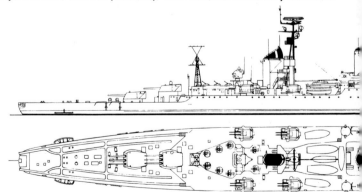

Krushchev stopped the programme. The later ships have a slightly differently arranged light anti-aircraft armament. *Ordzhonikidze* was transferred to Indonesia and renamed *Irian* in 1962, but she proved a white elephant and was later returned and scrapped. *Dzerzhinski* was fitted with an SAN-2 Guideline SAM twin launcher in place of X turret in 1961, and both *Admiral Senyavin* and *Zhdanov* were fitted with a SAN-4 SAM twin retractable launcher in place of X turret, an altered light anti-aircraft gun armament and improved communications facilities in 1972. Both can operate a helicopter, and *Admiral Senyavin* has had Y turret removed, X turret being replaced by a hangar. They are the Russian equivalent of the American converted *Cleveland* class light cruisers, now used as flagships.

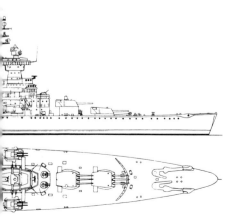

Above: The *Sverdlov* class cruiser *Aleksandr Suvorov* photographed in the Philippine Sea during the world-wide exercise 'Okean'. Although these ships are now rather elderly they are still being modified, indicating an intention to keep them in service for some years to come. Of great interest in this. picture is the stabilised 100mm gun turret on the starboard side which has either jammed or is being tilted for maintenance.

Yankee Class

Nuclear-powered ballistic missile submarines
34 boats.

Country of origin: Soviet Union
Displacement: 7800 tons surfaced (9300 tons submerged).
Dimensions: Length overall 427.8ft (129.5m); beam 38ft (11.6m); draught 25.6ft (7.8m).
Armament: Sixteen SLBMs, either SS-N-6 Mod 1 or Mod 3 (see text). One boat has twelve SS-N-17.
Propulsion: One nuclear reactor, two steam turbines (30,000shp), twin shafts; 20kts surfaced, 30kts submerged.

The *Yankee* class were the first Russian purpose-designed nuclear ballistic missile submarines to enter service, and (a decade after the Americans) they were the first Russian submarines to use hull-mounted SLBMs. The 16 missiles are arranged in two vertical rows of eight abaft the fin in a similar fashion to the American *Polaris* boats. The first twenty boats are armed with the SS-N-6 Mod 1 SLBM (NATO designation: SAWFLY). This has a single 1-2MT warhead and a range of some 1300 miles (1100nm). The next thirteen boats mount the longer range SS-N-6 Mod 3 which has three re-entry vehicles, not, however, independently targeted. It is not certain whether the SS-N-6 Mod 1 and Mod 3 are interchangeable. The least of the *Yankee* boats mount 12 of the newer SS-N-17 SLBMs, which have a range of 2400 miles, although this may have been a trial installation only. As with all Russian submarines they are noisier than their Western equivalents, and correspondingly easier to detect. The relatively short range of the SSN-6, even in its later variants, means that the *Yankees* must approach the American coast before launching their missiles, but the ability to launch the SS-N-6 submerged makes the *Yankees* considerably less vulnerable than previous Russian ballistic missile submarines.

Below: The *Yankee* class were the first Soviet submarines able to fire ballistic missiles while still submerged. There are 16 missiles mounted vertically in two rows of eight abaft the fin.

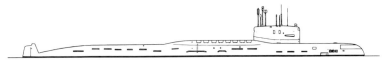

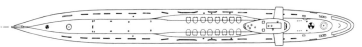

Above: *Yankee* class nuclear-powered ballistic missile submarine.

Above: This fine photo shows the casing covering the missiles (abaft the fin) which gives rise to considerable noise when underwater, thus making the boat easier to detect by NATO ships.

Descubierta Class

Frigates

Eight ships including *Descubierta* (F-81); *Diana* (F-82); *Infanta Elena* (F-83); *Infanta Cristina* (F-84).

Country of origin: Spain.
Displacement: 1233 tons (1479 full load).
Dimensions: Length overall 291·3ft (88·8m); beam 34ft·(10·4m); draught 11·1ft (3·2m).
Armament: Two four-cell Harpoon SSM launchers, one octuple Sea Sparrow launcher; one 3in (76mm) gun, two 40mm single Bofors guns; one 375mm Bofors twin-barrel rocket launcher; two triple tubes for Mk46 torpedoes.
Propulsion: Four diesels (16,000bhp), twin shafts; 25·5kts.

The Spanish Navy, which had been brought up to date in the early 1960s by the transfer of American vessels and the fitting of American weapons and electronics on to its warships, began a programme of re-equipping with new ships in the late 1960s. *Baleares* class frigates have been built since 1968 at Bazan's Ferrol yard. These are based on the US *Knox* class frigates, and have a standard displacement of 2,900 tons. For a modern small frigate design they have adopted the *Descubierta* class, a modified version of the Portuguese *Joao Coutinho* class. Three of the latter were built at the Spanish Bazan yard between 1968 and 1971, and three more by the German firm of Blohm und Voss. These have a standard displacement of 1.252 tons (1.272 tonnes) and are unsophisticated ships, with an armament of one twin 3in (76mm), a twin 40mm and a Hedgehog A/S projector. They also have a helicopter pad aft. Four of an improved version, the *Joao Robys* have also been built at Bazan for Portugal. These have a French 3·9in (100mm) gun and improved electronics. The Spanish ships have a similar but slightly larger hull, and they are faster and more sophisticated vessels, with a much improved armament. The single 3in (76mm) is mounted forward and the two 40mm in single mounts on the deckhouse aft. The Bofors A/S launcher is in 'B' position and the BPDMS Sea Sparrow launcher is fitted right aft. The funnel is split into two uptakes to avoid fume damage to the radar on the mainmast. These small and relatively cheap vessels are ideal for smaller navies which cannot afford the more sophisticated vessels adopted

by the major navies. They are capable of coping with most threats short of a major surface warship or a nuclear submarine, and the lack of more elaborate equipment means that the maintenance load is reduced. The *Descubiertas* were completed with SSMs, which has given them an anti-surface capability.

Above: *Descubierta,* **lead ship of a class of 8 under construction for the Royal Spanish Navy. They are similar to the Portuguese** *'Improved Jao Coutinho'* **class, but with much improved armament, more powerful engines and 'Y-funnel'. These interesting and cost-effective frigates are built by Bazan at Cartagena and Ferrol.**

Below: This model shows the unusual 'Y-funnel' which is designed to lead the fumes clear of the radar on the mainmast. The ships are fitted with the Selenia Albatros weapons system, which is designed for defence against aircraft and anti-ship missiles, as well as carrying out surface engagements with missiles and guns.

Spica Class

Fast attack craft
Spica class: 6 craft. *T-131* class: 12 craft.

Country of origin: Sweden.
Displacement: 200 tons (230 full load).
Dimensions: Length overall 134.5ft (41m); beam 23.3ft (7.1m); draught 5.2ft (1.6m).
Armament: One 57mm Bofors gun; six 21in (533mm) single torpedo tubes.
Propulsion: Three Rolls Royce Proteus (12,900bhp), three shafts; 40.5kts.

Like most other Baltic navies, the Swedish Navy now consists mainly of small submarines and missile and torpedo-armed patrol boats. The shallow seas, many islands and dominance of land-based aircraft in the area put a premium on small size, speed and an effective anti-aircraft armament. The use of gas turbines gives the *Spicas* a high speed and rapid acceleration, and the bridge is sited aft in order to give the 57mm anti-aircraft gun as large a field of fire as possible. This very effective Swedish-built weapon has a rate of fire of 200 rounds per minute, with a high rate of traverse and elevation, and the Swedish Navy considers it more effective than a missile in the anti-aircraft role. It can also be used against surface targets. It is controlled by the S62 combined search and target designation radar, mounted in a fibreglass dome on the bridge. The torpedoes are wire-guided. Twelve improved *Spica IIs* have been built between 1973 and 1976 with a modified hull and separate search and target designation radars. The Swedes have not adapted the *Spicas* to carry missiles, preferring to use a modified Norwegian design with 'Penguin' SSMs. However, the Danes are producing 10 modified *Spicas,* the *Willemoes* class, at the Royal Dockyard, Copenhagen. These are armed with Harpoon SSMs and wire-guided 21in (533mm) torpedoes, as well as a 3in (76mm) Oto Melara Compact gun. The bridge is much further forward on this class. The *Spicas* and their derivatives have a long and relatively narrow Lürssen-type hull, which is better suited to Baltic conditions than the beamier hull used in British designs. Four *Spicas* with MTV diesels are building for Malaysia. Over the years the Swedes have built a number of rock shelters along their coastline to act as 'hangars' for vessels up to the size of destroyers. These are capable of withstanding most weapons apart from atomic bombs, and considerably increase the survivability of the Swedish Navy.

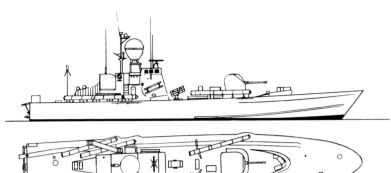

Above: The Swedish *Spica* class torpedo boat; 230 tons (234 tonnes).

Above: *Spica T121* torpedo boat. This is the original Spica type. Note the M22 radome for the M22 fire-control system.

Below: *Strömstad* (T-141) of the *Spica T131* class, a developed version of the original *Spicas.* Top speed is 40.5 knots.

Amazon Class

Frigates
Eight ships

Country of origin: United Kingdom.
Displacement: 2750 tons (3250 full load).
Dimensions: Length overall 384ft (117m); beam 40·5ft (12·3m); draught 19ft (5·8m).
Aircraft: One Westland Lynx helicopter.
Armament: Surface-to-air missiles, one quad Sea Cat launcher; surface-to-surface missiles, four Exocet launchers (*Amazon* and *Antelope* to be fitted at first major refit); main gun, one 4·5in Mk8 turret; AA guns, two 20mm Oerlikon; two triple torpedo tubes for Mk48 torpedoes.
Propulsion: Two Rolls Royce Olympus gas turbines (56,000bhp), two Rolls Royce Tyne gas turbines for cruising (8500shp), two shafts; 30kts full speed, 18kts on Tynes.

Before the first of the 'broad-beamed' *Leander* frigates was laid down discussion was afoot in the Admiralty about the *Leanders'* successor, and Vosper-Thorneycroft received a contract for a new design to be prepared in collaboration with Yarrow. They produced the *Amazon* class (Type 21), the first being laid down in November 1969. The variations from the *Leander*

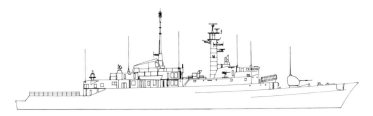

Above: Sleek outline of the *Amazon* class frigates.

design are interesting, while their hull-form and outline are attractive. The propulsion is gas-turbine which is likely to be used in all future British frigates. One helicopter is carried, and armament comprises one 4.5in (114mm) main gun, four Exocet surface-to-surface missiles, one Sea Cat SAM launcher and two 20mm Oerlikons. Despite this heavy armament the complement is 95 less than for the broad-beamed *Leanders*. Eight *Amazons* have been built and their successors will be the *Broadsword* (Type 22) class. ▶

Below: HMS *Alacrity*, sixth of eight *Amazon* class frigates, in the Clyde. All the Type 21s have Exocet and Seacat SSMs, although it was once planned to fit the last four with Seawolfs.

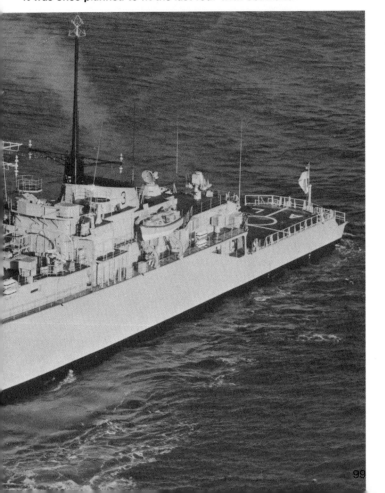

The Type 21 frigates were the first commercially designed ships to be accepted by the Royal Navy for many years. HMS *Amazon* (F-169) seen here shows off the superb lines and balance achieved by the designers at Yarrow. It is reported that despite having accepted the design the official departments obliged the firm to make many detailed alterations which delayed completion.

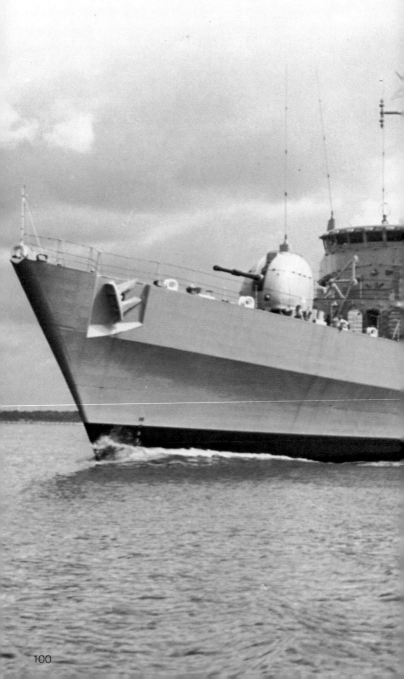

Broadsword Class

Frigates

One ship (four more planned): *Broadsword.*

Country of origin: United Kingdom.
Displacement: 3500 tons (4000 full load).
Dimensions: Length overall 430ft (131·2m); beam 48·5ft (14·8m); draught 14ft (4·3m).
Aircraft: Two Westland Lynx helicopters.
Armament: Four Exocet SSM launchers, two 6-barrelled Sea Wolf SAM launchers; two 40mm AA guns; two triple tubes for Mk46 torpedoes.
Propulsion: Two Rolls Royce Olympus gas turbines (56,000bhp), two Rolls Royce Tyne gas turbines. (8500bhp), two shafts; 30+kts.

Below: HMS *Broadsword* (F-88), the first of the Type 22s, successor to the *Leander* class which has served the Royal Navy so well. At least nine of this class will be built, with the fifth and subsequent ships being lengthened by some 20ft (6.1m).

Britain has had an outstanding success with its *Leander* class frigates which have served the Royal Navy well and sold widely overseas. The successor to the *Leander* is the *Broadsword* and the first of class was commissioned on 21 February 1979. The next four (*Battleaxe, Brilliant,* and two so far unnamed) will follow at yearly intervals thereafter.

These ships are powered by the now-familiar arrangement of two Rolls Royce Olympus gas turbines (56,000bhp) main engines and two Rolls Royce Tyne gas turbines (8500bhp) for economical cruising. This combination gives a top speed of over 30kts and a maximum range of 4500 miles (7242km) on the Tynes.

The *Broadwords* have a token gun armament of two 40mm guns and their main armament is all missiles, the first major Royal Navy class to attempt this transition. They are optimised for anti-submarine work with two triple tubes for Mk46 torpedoes and Type 2016 and Variable Depth sonars. The ships can carry two Westland Lynx helicopters, but it is understood that normally only one will be carried in peace.

As has happened with both the *Leander* and *Sheffield* classes the Royal Navy has decided to enlarge these latest ships and the fifth and subsequent ships will be some 20ft (6.1m) longer, making them virtually as big as the Soviet *Kynda* class, which are classified as cruisers. **continued ▶**

HMS *Broadsword* at sea off Portsmouth. Four
Exocet launchers are mounted on the foredeck,
with two 6-barrel Sea Wolf SAM launchers on
the upper deck—one before the bridge and the
second on top of the helicopter hangar aft.
Also visible here is one of the two 40mm guns
and in front of it a chaff dispenser.

County Class

Guided missile destroyers

8 ships: Group 1 (4 ships), including *Hampshire* (D-08);
and Group 2 (4 ships), including *Antrim* (D-18); *Fife* (D-20).

Country of origin: United Kingdom.
Displacement: 5440 tons (6200 full load).
Dimensions: Length overall 520·5ft (158·7m); beam 54·0ft (16·5m); draught 16·8ft (5·1m).
Aircraft: One Wessex.
Armament: Four Exocet missiles (except *Kent* and *London*), two 4·5in (114mm) twin guns, Seaslug SAM launchers (36 missiles carried), two quad Sea Cat launchers.
Propulsion: Two sets geared steam turbines (30,000shp), four gas turbines (30,000shp), two shafts; 30kts.

The *Countys* were intended primarily for AA defence of carrier task forces; and were designed round the Sea Slug SAM. Development of this medium range beam riding missle started in 1949, and a number of designs, including one for a 17,000 ton (17,270 tonne) cruiser, were prepared to carry it. However, a smaller cheaper ship was eventually selected, with two twin 4-5in (114mm) gun turrets forward to provide surface and shore bombardment capability. The *Countys* have a hangar and landing deck for a Wessex hunter-killer A/S helicopter, and mount a Sea Cat SAM quadruple launcher either side of the superstructure aft for close range AA defence. They are fully air-conditioned for defence against nuclear fall-out, and were the first major warships to have COSAG machinery. This enables them to get underway almost immediately, as well as providing rapid acceleration. The first four *Countys* were fitted with Sea Slug Mk I SAMs. They have the Type 965 single aerial air search radar on the mainmast, which is mounted further aft on *Kent* (D-12) and *London* (D-16) than on *Devonshire* (D-02) and *Hampshire* (D-08). The last four *Countys* have Sea Slug Mk 2 SAMs which have a limited SSM capability. They have the Type 965M double aerial on the mainmast. Because of Britain's economic situation and the decline of her carrier and seaborne assault forces, the first four *Countys* have not been given a mid-life refit, and are being discarded. However, *Norfolk* (D-21) was fitted with Exocet SSM launchers in place of B turret in 1974 to allow her to operate alone against major surface warships, and the other three ships in the second group are being similarly refitted. The *Countys* were to have

Below: The dramatic lines of the *County* class are shown by HMS *Kent* (D-12). This ship retains the second twin 4.5in (114mm) turret. *Hampshire* was paid off in 1976 and *Devonshire* in 1978.

Above: HMS *Norfolk* (D-21). Four single-cell Exocet SSM launchers have replaced 'B'-turret, but no reloads are carried. 36 Seaslug SAMs are carried and there are two quad Seacat SAM launchers.

been followed by the *Type 82* guided missle destroyers. These three funnel 5,650 ton (5,740 tonne) standard displacement ships were designed round the smaller, more capable Sea Dart SAM, with a single 4.5in (114mm) Mk 8 mount and an Ikara ASM launcher forward. Their immense cost and the cancellation of the aircraft carrier *CVA-01* meant that only one *Type 82*, *Bristol* (D-23), was completed.

Invincible Class

Through-deck cruisers

Two ships (one more forecast): *Invincible* (CAH-1); *Illustrious* (CAH-2).

Country of origin: United Kingdom.
Displacement: 16,000 tons (19,500 full load).
Dimensions: Length overall 677ft (206·6m); deck width overall 104·6ft (31·9m); beam 90ft (27·5m); draught 24ft (7·3m).
Aircraft: 10 Sea King, 8 Sea Harrier.
Armament: Twin Sea Dart SAM launchers.
Propulsion: Four Rolls Royce Olympus gas turbines. Total 112,000shp on two shafts; maximum speed 28kts.

The British withdrawal from the Mediterranean and from east of Suez, the cancellation of the large carrier *CVA-01* and the associated transfer of responsibility for maritime air roles to the (land-based) Royal Air Force in the mid-1960s left British naval planning in some disarray. However, a definite requirement still existed for vessels capable of operating and maintaining a number of ASW helicopters to counter the ever increasing threat from Russian submarines. As an interim measure two of the three *Tiger* class cruisers were converted between 1965 and 1972. They had been laid down as conventional *Swiftsure* class cruisers in 1941-1942, but were suspended at the end of World War II and not finally completed until 1959—1961. They were armed with the complex and unreliable automatic 6in (152mm) and 3in (76mm) mounts. *Tiger* (C-20) and *Blake* (C-99) had their aft twin 6in (152mm) turret replaced by a hangar and flight deck capable of operating four Sea King ASW helicopters. These conversions were very costly for the limited results achieved, so *Lion* (C-34) was scrapped without being converted. The definitive ASW design was *Invincible* (CAH-1). Political and ▶

Right: HMS *Invincible* (CAH-1) the Royal Navy's new light aircraft carrier. Note the interim ski-jump.

Below: A pilot's view of the flight-deck of *Invincible;* the designation 'through-deck cruiser' was a political dodge.

financial considerations delayed her order, but this was finally confirmed on 17 April 1973. Even after this date she has been delayed by financial stringency, and the MM-38 Exocet SSM quadruple-launcher was deleted She is much the same size as the *Majestic* class light fleet carriers, and is the largest warship laid down in Britain since World War II. She mounts a Sea Dart SAM twin-launcher on the fo'c's'le just forward of the flight deck in a position giving clear arcs of fire in most directions. There is a long island with two masts and funnels, and she has a clear flight deck angled slightly to port of the centrally mounted Sea Dart SAM launcher. There are two lifts, but she has no catapults or arrester-wires. She is the first large Western warship to be powered by gas turbines — the Tynes are for cruising and the Olympus engines provide full power. The clear flight deck was designed to enable the *Invincibles* to operate V/STOL aircraft as well as ASW helicopters. For several years this was not considered possible for political reasons, because of the decision to transfer maritime air roles to the Royal Air Force, and this capability was thinly disguised by the designation through-deck cruiser. However, the advantages of carrier-borne aircraft, including the much quicker reaction times possible, eventually proved unanswerable, and when *Invincible* (CAH-1) enters service she will operate a mixed complement of Sea King ASW helicopters and Sea Harrier V/STOL aircraft. Although the *Invincibles* are roughly similar in size to the Russian *Moskvas*, their aircraft are much more versatile despite the ships' smaller armament. The projected French nuclear-powered PA-75 type helicopter carriers will be very similar in all respects except for the type of machinery. In the gap between *Ark Royal* (R-09) having been phased out in 1978 and *Invincible* (CAH-1) entering service in 1980 her place has been taken by *Hermes* (R-12).

Above: HMS *Invincible* from above. The Royal Navy really wanted a larged fixed-wing carrier, the CVA-01, but this was turned down because of its great costs and large manpower requirement. Forced to compromise, a large helicopter carrier was designed, which by chance turned out to be suitable for V/STOL. Then a RN officer designed the ski-jump which, after a long struggle, the Admiralty was forced to accept. By such a process Britain has got just the ship needed for the 1980s!

Left: One twin Sea Dart SAM launcher, seen here on the fore-deck. The 7° ski-jump on this ship will be replaced by a full 15° on the next two: *Illustrious* and *Ark Royal*.

Leander Class

Frigates

UK 16 original and 10 broad-beamed ships, Australia 2 basically original
ships, Chile 2 broad-beamed ships, India 6 modified broad-beamed ships,
Netherlands 6 modified original ships, New Zealand 1 broad-beamed and 1
original ship.

Broad-beamed Leander:
Country of origin: United Kingdom.
Displacement: 2500 tons (2962 full load).
Dimensions: Length overall 372ft (113·4m); beam 43ft (13·1m); draught
18ft (5·5m).
Aircraft: One Westland Wasp with AS torpedoes (Lynx in *Phoebe* and
Sirius).
Armament: Depends upon 'group'. 'Ikara' group has two quad Sea Cat
SAM launchers, two 40mm AA guns and Ikara AS system; 'Exocet' group
has four Exocet launchers, two 40mm AA guns, three quad Sea Cat
launchers and two triple torpedo tubes; 'Broad-beamed' group has two
4·5in guns, two 20mm Oerlikon, and Limbo mortar (but see text for broad-
beamed conversions).
Propulsion: Two geared turbines (30,000shp), two shafts; 27kts.

Postwar building of frigates by the Royal Navy began in 1952 after a
considerable programme of conversions of the wartime construction
destroyers. Forty-eight of these had been built—of the survivors 33 became
Type 15 (full conversion) and seven of the T class, Type 16 (limited
conversions). In this period designs had been prepared of the Type 12
(general-purpose *Whitby* class, six ships), Type 14 (*Blackwood* class, 2nd
Rate, 12 ships), Type 41 (*Leopard* class, A/A frigates, 4 ships) and Type 61
(*Salisbury* Class, air direction frigates, four ships). The first of the Type 14
and Type 61 were laid down in 1952 and the total of 26 ships was completed

F 52

114

Above: *Leander* class; original gun-armed version with twin 4.5in.

between 1955 and 1960. The 1954-55 programme allowed for the first of nine ships of a modified Type 12, the *Rothesay* class, all of which were completed in 1960-61, being followed in 1961-64 by the seven Type 81 ships, the *Tribal* class. These were a new departure in having combined steam and gas turbine propulsion, although with only one screw and a speed of 28kts. A certain specialisation was evident here: the *Tribals* were intended primarily for Persian Gulf service, although when the last was completed in 1964 there would be only three more years of that requirement. On 10 April 1959 the first *Leander* was laid down. Although the *Rothesays* were converted to carry a helicopter the new class was the first British frigate designed to do so. With improved radar and variable depth sonar, this was the most numerous single class to be built for the Royal Navy for many years. In the 1964-65 programme the first of the 'broad-beamed' variety was allowed for. These, the last ten of the class, were 2ft (0.6m) broader to improve stability. Rearmament programmes were begun in 1971 when the first Ikara conversion (*Leander*) was put in hand. Seven more followed. The conversion involved the replacement of the 4.5in (114mm) turret by the A/S launcher, and a similar loss took place in the Exocet conversion, the first (of 8) of which, *Cleopatra,* was completed in November 1975. It is of interest that the Chilean *Leanders* have also received Exocet, but not at the expense of the turret.

The 'broad-beamed' *Leanders* are also being converted, starting with *Andromeda,* and they will all be fitted with four Exocet, the Sea Wolf SAM system, and improved electronics. The 4.5in turret, Sea Cat launcher and Limbo mortar will all be removed.

Left: HMS *Juno* (F-52) of the extremely successful *Leander* class. 44 of these ships have been built for six navies. *Juno* is one of eight being rearmed with Exocet SSM; she recommissions in 1980.

Oberon Class and Porpoise Class

Submarines

35 boats: *Oberon class* (27 boats): 13RN including *Oberon* (S-09); *Onyx* (S-21); 6 RAN including *Oxley* (S-57); *Ovens* (S-70); 3 Brazilian Navy including *Humaita* (S-20); *Riachuela* (S-22); 3 RCN including *Ojibwa* (OS-72); *Okanagan* (SS-74); and 2 Chilean Navy *O'Brien* (S-22); *Hyatt* (S-23). *Porpoise class* (8 boats): including *Porpoise* (S-01); *Sea Lion* (S-07).

Country of origin: United Kingdom.
Displacement: 1610 tons surfaced (2410 tons submerged).
Dimensions: Length overall 295·2ft (73·5m); beam 26·5ft (8·1m); draught 18ft (5·5m).
Armament: Eight 21in (533mm) torpedo tubes.
Propulsion: Two Admiralty standard diesels; 6000shp; 17kts. submerged.

After 1945 Britain ran trials with a number of ex-German submarines including the Type XVIIB *Meteorite* (ex *U-1407)* which was powered by a hydrogen-peroxide fuelled Walter turbine. Two British hydrogen-peroxide fuelled experimental submarines, *Explorer* (S-30) and *Excalibur* (S-40), ran trials between 1956 and 1965 but this fuel was too dangerous for normal use, and the first British postwar operational submarines, the *Porpoise* class, combined the best features of conventional British and German wartime designs. They have a semi-streamlined hull, and are extremely quiet, with an excellent range and habitability and a deep designed diving depth. Some of the class have been discarded before the planned date to allow more money and men to be allocated to the nuclear submarine programme. The *Oberons* are virtually repeat *Porpoises* with improved equipment and a glass fibre

Above: *Oberon* class. Note clean lines, bow sonar and tall fin.

superstructure fore and aft of the conning tower in all except *Orpheus* which uses light alloy aluminium. A number of these excellent submarines have been supplied to other navies, but problems with the electric cables have delayed the Chilean and last two Australian ships. *Oberon* has been modified to carry equipment to train crews for the nuclear submarines.

Although nuclear submarines are superior to conventional boats in most respects, the nuclear boats are many times more expensive and only major powers can afford them.

Above: A *Porpoise* class submarine on the surface. These versatile and successful boats have served for some 20 years in five navies; the Royal Navy has scrapped one (*Rorqual*) and placed a further four in reserve. A new class of non-nuclear boats will be built to replace them.

Left: HMS *Osiris* of the *Oberon* class. She has eight torpedo tubes (six bow, two stern) and carries a total of 24 21 inch (533mm) homing torpedoes. These submarines are fast, very quiet and difficult to detect, and are by no means superseded by nuclear boats. The picture shows the clean lines needed for quiet running underwater.

Resolution Class

Nuclear-powered ballistic missile submarines

Four boats: *Resolution* (S-22); *Renown* (S-26); *Repulse* (S-23); *Revenge* (S-27).

Country of origin: United Kingdom.
Displacement: 7500 tons surfaced (8400 tons submerged).
Dimensions: Length overall 425ft (129·5m); beam 33ft (10·1m); draught 30ft (9·1m).
Armament: Submarine-launched ballistic missiles, sixteen vertically-launched Polaris A3; torpedo tubes, six 21in in bow.
Propulsion: One Rolls Royce pressurised water-cooled reactor, one set English Electric steam turbines; 25kts submerged.

In the late 1950s it had been planned that the Royal Air Force would provide the British strategic deterrent in the 1960s and 1970s using 'V' bombers armed with Skybolt, a stand-off missile then under development in the USA. However, at the Nassau Conference in 1962 President Kennedy told Britain that America was unilaterally abandoning the Skybolt project because of development difficulties. It was decided at that conference that Britain should build her own nuclear ballistic missile submarines. The Polaris SLBMs would be provided by the United States, but Britain would fit her own warheads.

Four submarines were commenced, and when *Resolution* was laid down in February 1964 it was announced that a fifth Polaris submarine was to be ordered. This would ensure that one would always be available on patrol, but this boat was cancelled in 1965 as part of the Labour government's cost cutting defence review.

A good deal of technical assistance was obtained from the Americans, and the *Resolutions* are very similar to the American *Lafayette* class Polaris submarines. The *Resolutions'* actual design is based on that of the *Valiant*

Above: The nuclear-powered ballistic missile submarine (SSBN) HMS *Resolution* exhausting air from her tanks before diving. She carries sixteen Polaris A-3 missiles with a range of 2500miles.

(S102) with a missile compartment between the control centre and the reactor room. *Resolution's* Polaris A3 missiles have a range of 2,500 miles (2,102nm) and are each fitted with ten 60 kiloton MRV warheads in British designed re-entry vehicles. Various proposals to replace the now obsolescent Polaris with Poseidon have been abandoned as a result of financial and political considerations. However, development is continuing on the existing delivery system and warheads to ensure their viability into the 1980s.

Below: HMS *Repulse* at speed on the surface. The Royal Navy had planned to build five of these SSBNs in order to be able to guarantee a minimum of one on patrol at any one time, which is necessary if deterrence is to be credible. Unfortunately the plan to build the fifth was cancelled in February 1965.

Sheffield Class

Guided missile destroyers

12 ships: Britain 10+ ships including *Sheffield* (D-80);
and Argentina 2 ships, *Hercules* (D-01); *Santissima Trinidad* (D-02).

Country of origin: United Kingdom.
Displacement: 3150 tons (4100 full load).
Dimensions: Length overall 410ft (125m), beam 47ft (14.3m), draught 12.5ft (3.8m).
Aircraft: One Lynx Mk2 Helicopter.
Armament: One twin Sea Dart SAM launcher, one 4.5in (115mm) main gun, two 20mm Oerlikon, two triple tubes for Mk46 torpedoes.
Propulsion: Two Rolls Royce Olympus gas turbines (50,000shp), two Rolls Royce Tyne (8000shp) for cruising; 30kts.

The *County* class destroyers were to have been followed by the *Type 82* guided missile destroyers. These three-funnel 5,650 ton (5,740 tonnes) standard displacement ships were designed round the smaller, more capable Sea Dart SAM, with a single 4.5in (114mm) Mk 8 mount and an Ikara ASM launcher forward. Their immense cost and the cancellation of the aircraft carrier *CVA-01* meant that only one *Type 82, Bristol* (D23) was completed. The *Sheffield* class were designed as cheaper, smaller and less sophisticated versions of *Bristol*, but are still complex and highly automated vessels. They have COGOG machinery and they have a hangar and flight-deck aft for a Lynx A/S helicopter. The Sea Dart SAM has a limited SSM capability and the single launcher is fitted forward between the gun mount and the bridge. Later ships of this class will be completed to a rather different design, with the beam increased by 2ft (0.609m) and the length by 53ft (15.9m), although it is reported that displacement will not be affected. The unsightly exhausts fitted to *Sheffield's* funnel to overcome efflux problems have now been removed.

Below: HMS *Sheffield*, name ship of the class, was laid down in January 1970, launched in June 1971 and commissioned in 1975. The larger Soviet *Kiev* carriers took only two years to fit out.

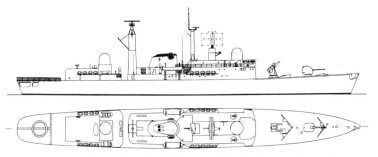

Above: Note the 115mm (4.5in) gun and twin Sea Dart launcher.

Above: *Birmingham* (D-86). Main AS weapon system is the Westland Lynx helicopter armed with Mark 44 torpedoes or Sea Skua ASMs.

Swiftsure Class

Fleet submarines

Five boats (one more planned): *Swiftsure; Sovereign; Superb; Sceptre; Spartan.*

Country of Origin: United Kingdom.
Displacement: 4200 tons surfaced (4500 tons submerged).
Dimensions: Length overall 272ft (82.9), beam 32.3ft (9.8m); draught 27ft (8.2m).
Armament: Five 21in (533mm) torpedo tubes.
Propulsion: One pressurised water-cooled nuclear reactor; English Electric steam turbines. (15,000shp), one Paxman auxiliary diesel (4,000hp), one shaft; Submerged speed 30kts.

The British nuclear submarine programme started with *Dreadnought* which was laid down in 1959 and commissioned on 17 April 1963. She has a British-designed hull, although the propulsion machinery was supplied by the United States in order to speed up the programme. This *Dreadnought* was as revolutionary to the Royal Navy as the previous *Dreadnought* was in

Below: A *Swiftsure* class nuclear-powered fleet submarine leaves her base in Scotland for a patrol in the Atlantic. The first boat of this class joined the fleet in 1973, but the sixth and last will not be operational until 1981 at the earliest.

1905 and she has given birth to a long line of nuclear-powered submarines.

Next to appear was the *Valiant* class of which the name ship was commissioned on 18 July 1966. This boat is of similar design to *Dreadnought*, although slightly larger and with a greater displacement (4900 tons submerged as opposed to 4000 tons for *Dreadnought*). *Valiant* also has more British equipment, Rolls Royce providing the nuclear plant, and English Electric the steam turbines and condensors. A notable demonstration was given in 1967 when *Valiant* made a submerged voyage from Singapore to England in 28 days without surfacing or refuelling. *Valiant* was followed by *Warspite, Churchill, Conqueror* and *Courageous.*

The next class to appear was the *Swiftsure* class, the first of which joined the fleet in April 1973. These boats are 13ft (4m) shorter than the *Valiants,* with a flat upper deck which gives a completely different appearance from the humped back of *Dreadnought* and the *Valiants.* This new shape is evidence of greater internal volume of the pressure hull leading to more space for equipment and better living conditions. There are five torpedo tubes, with 20 reloads.

The effectiveness of all these Fleet submarines will be greatly increased when the Sub-Harpoon anti-ship missile enters Royal Navy service in the early 1980s. There are five *Swiftsure* boats in service (*Swiftsure, Sovereign Superb, Sceptre* and *Spartan*) with a sixth due to be commissioned in 1981. These will be followed by the *Trafalgar* class of which two have so far been laid down. **continued ▶**

Below: A *Swiftsure* class submarine at speed on the surface. The shape of the hull is somewhat different from that of previous British SSNs and is indicative of greater internal volume, giving more space for equipment and for the crew.

The splendid lines and the very smooth outer casing of the *Swiftsure* class boats are essential for quietness, especially since these submarines are hunter/killers, whose task is to stalk enemy ballistic missile armed boats and destroy them if necessary before they can launch their deadly weapons against targets in the West.

Winchester SRN-6 Class

Hovercraft
20 craft: Britain 1 craft, Iran 8 craft. Egypt 3 craft; Saudi Arabia 8 craft.

Country of origin: United Kingdom.
Displacement: 6.33 tons (10 full load).
Dimensions: Length overall 48.4ft (14.7m); beam 25.3ft (7.7m); height 15.9ft (4.8m).
Armament: Can carry machine guns.
Propulsion: One Rolls Royce Gnome gas turbine (1400shp); 50kts.

The SRN-6 delivered to the Royal Navy trials unit in 1967 was designed by Saunders-Roe, and is a commercial passenger craft, although it has been modified with hardpoints to carry weapons and equipment. It is a larger version of the SRN-5, six of which were licence-built by Bell in America, three for the US Navy and three for the US Army. Designated the SK-5 Patrol Air-cushion Vehicle (AACV), they were armed with two 0.5in (12.7m) and two

0·3in (7·62mm) machine-guns and grenade launchers for their deployment in South Vietnam from 1968. Britain has also built a 50 ton (50·8 tonne) military hovercraft, the BH-7 *Wellington*, one of which was supplied to the Royal Navy in 1970, and six to Iran. They have a full load displacement of 50 tons (51 tonnes) and a speed of 60kts. These hovercraft can be used for a variety of roles, including minesweeping, troop-transport, and as patrol vessels, but they are complex and expensive and their only widespread use so far has been in the Middle East, where they are well suited to areas of desert and shallow water. The United States has built the Bell SES-100B 100 ton (102 tonne) craft, and may construct a 3,000 ton (3,050 tonne) LSES vessel. This will be an anti-submarine vessel, armed with guns, missiles and helicopters, but it will also be able to operate V/TOL aircraft. Her size will enable her to carry sufficient fuel for a reasonable range, and to operate in rough seas, thereby overcoming two restrictions on the employment of smaller hovercraft such as the 200 ton (203 tonne) British SRN-4, one of which was chartered in 1976 by the Royal Navy for minesweeping trials. The USSR also has a number of naval hovercraft, 33 of the *Gus* class 27 ton (27·4 tonne) craft, and 18 of 220 ton (224 tonne) vessels of the *Aist* class. Other types are under evaluation.

Left: An SRN-6 *Winchester* class hovercraft in the markings of the Royal Navy Hovercraft Trials Unit. Powered by a Rolls-Royce Gnome gas-turbine it has a speed of 50 knots. Although a British invention, and despite lengthy trials, the Royal Navy has still not found a proper role for the hovercraft.

Below: An SRN-5 motors up river in Borneo in the 'Confrontation' campaign with Indonesia; note the machine-gunner at the ready on the cabin roof. In jungle-covered terrain such as Borneo and South Vietnam the hover-craft was able to prove its worth.

Belknap Class

Cruisers
Nine ships including *Belknap* (CG-26), *Biddle* (CG-34).

Country of origin: United States
Displacement: 6,570 tons (7,930 full load).
Dimensions: Length overall 547ft (166·7m); beam 54ft 10in (16·7m); draught 28ft 10in (8·8m).
Aircraft: One Kaman SH-2F Seasprite with hangar and pad at aft end of superstructure.
Armament: Surface-to-air and AS missiles, one ASTOR (Standard and ASROC) twin launcher forward; guns, one single 5in 54-cal right aft, two single 3in one each side amidships; torpedo tubes, two triple Mk 32 12·7in (324mm) mounts one each side of the superstructure abreast the forward mack.
Propulsion: Two sets GE or De Laval steam turbines. Total 85,000shp on two shafts, maximum speed 34kts.

The *Belknap*s are the last conventionally powered US cruisers to be built up to the present. They are anti-aircraft and anti-submarine escorts for the US carriers and they have been developed from the smaller conventionally powered *Leahy*s. Like them, the *Belknap*s are long-ranged, seaworthy ships with sophisticated electronics, but these features have been attained at the expense of weapons systems. The most serious lack is the absence of an adequate SSM, though this is being remedied by the addition of Harpoon. By the time the *Belknap*s were designed, the USN had realized the advantages of carrying a helicopter on board, and they had also appreciated the continued advantages of guns. As a result, the *Leahy*s' aft Terrier SAM launcher was replaced by a 5in 54-cal gun and a pad and hangar for a helicopter. Space was also saved forward by firing ASROC ASMs from the same launcher as the SAMs. As in the Leahys, the two uptakes are incorporated into macks. Ten *Belknap* class Guided Missile Cruisers (CG) were to have been built, but as with the earlier class Congress insisted that one should be nuclear powered, so only nine conventionally powered *Belknap*s were built between 1962–67. Their nuclear powered half-sister, *Truxtun* (CGN-35), was built between 1963–67, and like *Bainbridge* (CGN-25) has two D2G reactors in a slightly larger hull. She differs from her conventionally powered half-sisters not only because she is nuclear powered and

Above: USS *Belknap* (CG-26). Note missile launcher forward, gun aft.

Above: The *Belknap* class was the last conventionally powered class of cruisers to be built for the US Navy, in 1962-1963.

has lattice masts instead of macks, but also because she has the 5in 54-cal gun on the forecastle and the SAM/ASM launcher on the quarterdeck. One problem with ships fitted with the joint SAM/ASM launcher is that if the launcher were damaged or broke down, the ship would be deprived of a large part of its AA and AS capability. *Belknap* (CG-26) was severely damaged in collision with the US carrier *John F Kennedy* (CV-67) in the Mediterranean on 22 November 1975. Her entire upperworks were removed by the carrier's overhang, and a serious fire followed. There was a possibility that she might be scrapped, but she is now being refitted with improved weapons systems.

Below: USS *Truxton* (CGN-35) was to have been conventionally powered, but the US Congress insisted on nuclear power for one.

Coontz Class

Destroyers

Ten ships including *Coontz* (DDG-40), *Dewey* (DDG-45).

Country of origin: United States
Displacement: 4,700 tons (5,800 full load).
Dimensions: Length overall 512ft 6in (156·2m); beam 52ft 6in (15·9m); draught 25ft (7·6m).
Armament: Surface-to-air missiles, one Terrier twin launcher right aft; guns, one single 5in 54-cal forward; AS weapons, one ASROC 8-tube launcher superimposed forward; torpedo tubes, two triple Mk 32 12·7in (324mm) mounts one each side between the funnels amidships.
Propulsion: Two sets De Laval or Allis Chalmers steam turbines. Total 85,000shp on two shafts, maximum speed 34kts.

The *Coontz* class were originally rated as Frigates (DLG), but they are now classified as Guided Missile Destroyers (DDG). They were the first American escorts to be designed to carry guided missiles, and are based on the earlier *Mitscher* class, which were armed with guns and AS weapons. The *Coontz* class were the only US Frigates to have separate masts and funnels, and are single-ended ships, with a 5in 54-cal gun and a superfiring ASROC ASM launcher forward and a twin Terrier SAM launcher aft. They were originally designed to have a second single 5in 54-cal gun in B position, but this was replaced by the ASROC launcher before they were laid down. As built, they had two twin 3in (76mm) mounts abaft the aft funnel, but these were removed when the class was modernized between 1968 and 1975. This was intended to improve their AA capabilities, and they have been fitted with Standard in place of Terrier SAMs, NTDS and improved radar. *King* (DLG-10, later DDG-41) and *Mahan* (DLG-11 later DDG-42) were used with the *Essex* class carrier *Oriskany* (CVA-34 later CV-34) as trials ships for NTDS in 1961–62. *King* was later used between 1973–74 for sea trials of the Vulcan–Phalanx 20mm CIWS (Close In Weapon System) gun. This class can be distinguished by the large superstructure and absence of a gun aft. Ten ships were built though it had originally been intended to

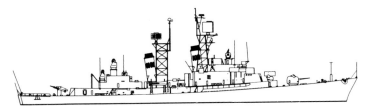

Above: *Coontz* class, first US escorts to carry guided missiles.

construct twenty. However improvements in weapon design and the introduction of macks meant that the class were curtailed, and the money allocated for the remaining ten went towards the completely redesigned *Leahy*s. As refitted the *Coontz* class are powerful AA and AS escorts, but they have only a limited surface capability and the lack of room for a hangar means that they cannot permanently embark a helicopter though one can be operated from the pad aft.

Above: USS *Coontz* (DDG-40). These ships were at first classified as Guided Missile Frigates (DLG) and when this picture was taken *Coontz* was designated DLG-9. They were reclassified in 1975 as DDGs.

Left: *USS Preble* **(DDG-46) of the *Coontz* class being replenished by a *Neosho* class oiler (AO). Note on *Preble* the 5in (127mm) gun and the ASROC launcher in front of the bridge. A basic limitation of this class is that, although there is a landing area for a helicopter on the stern, there is no hangar and support capability is limited.**

Enterprise Class

Aircraft carrier
One ship: *Enterprise* (CVN-65).

Country of origin: United States
Displacement: 75,700 tons (89,600 full load).
Dimensions: Length overall 1,102ft (335·9m); deck width overall 252ft (76·8m); beam 133ft (40·5m); draught 35·8ft (10·8m).
Aircraft: Over 90 aircraft and helicopters.
Armament: Surface-to-air missiles, two BPDMS Sea Sparrow 8-tube launchers on sponsons one each side aft.
Propulsion: Eight A2W reactors, four sets Westinghouse steam turbines. Total approx 280,000shp on four shafts, maximum speed approx 35kts.

USS *Enterprise* (CVN-65) was designed at a time when fierce argument was taking place in the USA over the future value of aircraft carriers, and she

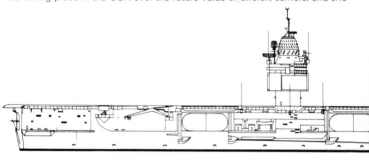

was commissioned in the first year of the Kennedy administration whose Secretary of Defense, Robert McNamara, was by no means convinced of the cost-effectiveness of a ship which had cost $451,300,000. Her hull design was a modification of that of the *Forrestal* class conventionally powered aircraft carriers but the inclusion of nuclear propulsion and other differences resulted in her being the largest warship built up to that time. With the cruiser *Long Beach* (CGN-9) completing shortly before her, *Enterprise* (CVN-65) was the second nuclear powered warship and probably the most distinctive. Having no requirement for funnel uptakes the bridge is box-shaped with a cone top. At the lower level "bill-board" fixed array radar antennae for the SPS 32 and 33 "3-D" sets are fitted to the sides and the cone is fitted with aerials for electronic counter-measures. The design of the nuclear plant was initiated in 1950, deferred from 1953–54 to obtain full value from developments in submarine nuclear propulsion, and then continued to the production stage by the Bettis Atomic Power

Below: USS *Enterprise* (CVN-65) was commissioned on 25 Nov 1961.

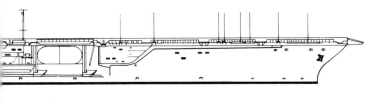

At the time of construction *Enterprise* was the largest warship ever built, and even now is only rivalled by the three *Nimitz* class carriers.

Laboratory. On 2 December 1960, just two months after launching, *Enterprise's* first reactor went critical, and in the next 11 months all eight, feeding 32 heat exchangers and with two reactors for each shaft, reached criticality. From her commissioning in November 1961 until her first refit and nuclear refuelling which started in November 1964 she steamed nearly 210,000 miles. With a range such as this, to be steadily and notably increased as future refuellings provide improved cores, with a higher speed than previous carriers and with 50 percent more aviation fuel than the *Forrestals*, stored in space taken up by the ship's own fuel in conventionally powered units, she proved many of the points advanced by the supporters of nuclear propulsion. But with over 90 aircraft and helicopters to operate and 5,500 men to be fed there is still the continual need for underway replenishment groups to provide fuel, munitions and food. Although the frequency of such replenishments is much less than the conventional weekly rendezvous with a tanker, under intensive operating it will still cause problems for planners. The requirement for ammunition and missiles for ship-board systems is, however, minimal as *Enterprise* (CVN-65) has no guns and, although allowance was originally made for a Terrier SAM system, her sole armament is a pair of BPDMS Sea Sparrow SAM launchers. Like all US carriers, she relies mainly on aircraft for long range defense and on escorts for close range protection. With the embarkation of AS aircraft, she was reclassified from CVAN to CVN on 30 June 1975.

Above: Critics of these 'super-carriers' query the wisdom of concentrating so many assets into one, not invulnerable, hull.

Below: The bridge structure of *Enterprise* is unique with its ECM dome and the SPS-32 and -33 'billboards'.

Forrestal Class

Aircraft carriers
Four ships: *Forrestal* (CV-59), *Saratoga* (CV-60), *Ranger* (CV-61), *Independence* (CV-62).

Country of origin: United States
Displacement: 60,000 tons (78,700 full load).
Dimensions: Length overall 1,039ft (316·8m); deck width overall 252ft (76·8m); beam 129ft 6in (39·5m); draught 37ft (11·3m).
Aircraft: Over 80 aircraft and helicopters.
Armament: Surface-to-air missiles, three BPDMS Sea Sparrow 8-tube launchers on sponsons one to starboard forward and one each side aft.
Propulsion: Four sets Westinghouse steam turbines. Total 280,000shp on four shafts, maximum speed 34kts.

United States (CVA-58), the first postwar American aircraft carrier to be laid down, had a designed displacement of 65,000 tons. She was to have had funnels flush with the flight deck and a retractable bridge to provide the maximum possible deck space for operating the large postwar carrier aircraft. However, she was cancelled almost immediately after being laid down in April 1949 because of doubts about her design and function, and because of pressure from the USAF Strategic Air Command. The subsequent "Admirals' revolt" and a reassessment of the value of aircraft carriers in the light of the Korean War resulted in the US Navy being allowed to build a fleet based on large aircraft carriers. A *Forrestal* was authorized each year from 1952–55, and *Forrestal* (CV-59), *Saratoga* (CV-60), *Ranger* (CV-61) and *Independence* (CV-62) were built between 1952–59. They were the

Right: USS *Forrestal* (CV-59) 79,300 tons full load displacement, was commissioned 1 Oct 1955.

Below: The *Forrestal* class introduced many new features: angled deck, steam catapults (both British inventions), and special underwater protection. They were the first carriers built specifically to operate jet aircraft.

largest aircraft carriers to be built since the Japanese *Shinano* of 1944. Their design was based on that of the *United States* (CVA-58), but it was modified to take advantage of the new British angled deck. This underwent very successful trials on the *Essex* class aircraft carrier *Antietam* (CV-36) in 1952, and gave the necessary deck space whilst still retaining a fixed island and funnel. *Forrestal* (CV-59) is the first American aircraft carrier to be built with an angled deck. This is angled at 8° and the flight deck and island are sponsoned out to twice the width of the hull. The four lifts, each 52ft 3in by 62ft (15·9m by 18·9m) are external to the hull, eliminating a source of weakness in previous carriers' flight decks. *Forrestal* (CV-59) is also the first American carrier to be built with steam catapults (another British invention), having two forward and two on the angled deck enabling four aircraft to be launched in very rapid succession. To improve seaworthiness the *Forrestals* have a fully enclosed hurricane bow, the first fitted to an American carrier since the pre-war *Lexingtons*. However, when first completed they were unable to maintain high speed in rough weather because the forward 5in gun sponsons were liable to structural damage because of their size and position. They were therefore removed, and most eight single 5in 54-cal have since been replaced by three BPDMS Sea Sparrow SAM launchers. Another weak point in the design is the positioning of the port lift at the forward end of the angled deck where it interferes with flying operations. *Saratoga* (CV-60), *Ranger* (CV-61) and *Independence* (CV-62) are slightly larger than *Forrestal*, and have more powerful engines giving a knot more speed. *Ranger* (CV-61) has a wider flight deck and *Independence* (CV-62) is slightly longer. The data applies to *Saratoga* (CV-60). Since the phasing out of the *Essex* class carriers, they all now operate a mix of fighter, attack, airborne radar, reconnaissance and AS aircraft and helicopters, and were reclassified from (CVA) to (CV) on 30 June 1975.

George Washington Class

Nuclear-powered ballistic missile submarines
Five boats including *George Washington* (SSBN-598),
Robert E Lee (SSBN 601).

Country of origin: United States
Displacement: 6,019 tons surface (6,888 submerged).
Dimensions: Length overall 381ft 8in (116·3m); beam 33ft (10·1m);
draught 29ft (8·8m).
Armament: Submarine launched ballistic missiles, sixteen vertical tubes
for Polaris A-3 in two rows of eight in hull behind fin; torpedo tubes, six 21in
(533m) in bow.
Propulsion: One Westinghouse S5W reactor, one set GE steam turbines.
Total 15,000shp on one shaft, submerged speed approximately 30kts.

In 1955 the Soviet Union began the conversion of six *Zulu* class conventionally powered submarines to fire ballistic missiles. The modification
involved the fitting of two launch tubes in the fin for the surface-discharged
300 mile range SSN-4 Snark SLBMs. A year earlier the USN had laid down
the first of two *Grayback* class conventionally powered submarines, firing
the Regulus I surface-launched cruise missile, and in 1957 laid down a
nuclear powered Regulus I submarine, *Halibut*, which entered service in
1960. However, at that time cruise missiles were considerably more
vulnerable than ballistic missiles, and in the early 1950s the US Navy, in
collaboration with the US Army, started development of the Jupiter ICBM.
This was to be fueled by liquid oxygen and kerosene, and three of these
monster 60ft (18·3m) surface-launched missiles were intended to be
carried in a 10,000 ton nuclear submarine. At the same time as the Russian
developments made a US ballistic missile submarine more urgently required,
developments in solid fuel and miniaturization had produced the Polaris
A-1 SLBM. Not only did this have solid fuel, with all its attendent advantages, it could be launched submerged and had a range of 1,380 miles
and it was so small that sixteen could be carried in the hull of a submarine
only half the size of the projected Jupiter armed SSBN. The submerged
launch capability and the for that period long range of the Polaris A-1
SLBM meant that the Polaris armed submarines were virtually undetectable
before they had launched their missiles, whereas their Russian contem-
poraries had to close virtually to American coastal waters and were forced
to surface to fire their missiles. In order to put Polaris into service as soon as
possible, the five *George Washington* class Nuclear Ballistic Missile
Submarines (SSBN) were basically lengthened versions of the *Skipjack*
class SSNs, *George Washington* (SSBN-598) herself was laid down as the

Above: The *Washington* class were the first Polaris missile boats.

nuclear attack submarine *Scorpion*, and was lengthened 130ft (40m) on the stocks. This additional section, which contained the launch tubes, was inserted immediately aft of the fin. The original powerplant and much of the attack submarine's equipment were retained in the SSBN. The five *George Washington*s, built between 1957–61, were in service for seven years before the first Russian equivalents, the *Yankee* class SSBNs, became operational. By the mid-1960s the relatively short range of the Polaris A-1 SLBMs, which restricted the waters that the SSBNs could operate in whilst still allowing their missiles to reach targets inside Russia, was making the *George Washington*s more vulnerable to Russian countermeasures. Therefore during their first recoring between 1964–67 the class were fitted with the 2,880 mile Polaris A-3 SLBM. Their electronics has also been upgraded.

Above: USS *George Washington* (SSBN-598). Note the teardrop hull, diving planes on fin and casing over Polaris missile tubes.

Below: The five submarines of the *George Washington* class were modified during 1964-67 to fire the improved Polaris A-3 missile but there are not any plans to modify them to take Poseidon.

Knox Class

Frigates
46 ships.

Country of origin: United States
Displacement: 3,011 tons (3,877 full load).
Dimensions: Length overall 438ft (133·5m); beam 46ft 9in (14·25m); draught 24ft 9in (7·6m).
Aircraft: Kaman SH-2F Seasprite helicopter with hangar and pad aft.
Armament: Surface-to-air missiles, one BPDMS Sea Sparrow 8-tube launcher right aft; guns, one single 5in 54-cal forward; AS weapons, one ASROC 8-tube launcher in front of bridge; torpedo tubes, four Mk 32 12·7in (324mm) tubes at stern.
Propulsion: One Westinghouse steam turbine. Total 35,000shp, maximum speed over 27kts.

The *Knox* class frigates are second generation US postwar escorts, and are the largest class of surface warships built in America since the war. The first generation postwar escorts were the *Dealey, Courtney* and *Claud Jones* classes, built between 1952–60. These are conventional turbine or diesel powered single-screw ships developed from World War II designs, but whereas the *Dealey*s and *Courtney*s were successful ships, too much was attempted on too small a displacement with the *Claud Jones* class, and a new type of ship was necessary. The first of the second-generation escorts are the *Bronstein* class, built between 1961–63. These are much larger ships with a new hull form, capable of carrying ASROC, DASH, a twin 3in (76mm) mount and modern electronics, including a bow sonar. To save deck space they have a mack. Two were built, and the ten *Garcia*s, an enlarged version built between 1962–68, have a similar layout but have a flush deck and two single 5in (127mm) guns. They introduced the very high pressure boilers, which save space and weight. Six *Brooke*s, a version with an improved anti-aircraft armament, were also built. A Tartar SAM single launcher replaced the aft 5in (127mm) gun, but this proved too expensive. The *Knox* class, forty-six of which have been built between 1965–74, are very similar but slightly larger than the *Garcia*s. Originally intended to mount the cancelled "Sea Mauler" short range SAM, some now have a BPDMS Sea Sparrow SAM launcher instead. In some ships the ASROC AS launcher can fire RIM-24B Tartar SSMs, conferring a surface offensive capability. Harpoon SSMs are now being retrofitted. The last 20 ships, built under a Total Procurement Contract by the Avondale Shipyards, Westwego, were at first known as the *Joseph Hewes* class, although they are virtually identical to the other *Knox*s. Like all US escorts with the new hull form, the *Knox*s are extremely seaworthy, but the single engine and shaft makes them vulnerable to damage or breakdown. However, this reflects the US wartime experience that it is engine rather than ship production that causes bottlenecks in the supply of escorts.

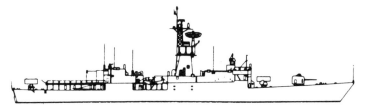

Above: *Knox* class. 46 ships commissioned 1969-1974.

Above: USS *Knox* (FF-1052). The 46 ships of the *Knox* class are the largest group of major surface warships built to the same design since the end of World War II.

Below left: USS *Bronstein* (FF-1037), one of a two-ship class which were the first of the 'second-generation' frigates of the USN, and were developed through *Garcia* and *Brooke* to *Knox* class.

Below: USS *Garcia* (FF-1040). Following the *Bronstein* class came the ten *Garcias* with a flush deck and two single 5in (127mm) guns. They can also operate an SH-2D helicopter (LAMPS).

Long Beach Class

Cruiser
One ship: *Long Beach* (CGN-9)

Country of origin: United States
Displacement: 14,200 tons (17,100 full load).
Dimensions: Length overall 721ft 2in (220m); beam 73ft 2in (22·3m); draught 31ft (9·5m).
Aircraft: One Kaman SH-2F Seasprite on pad right aft.
Armament: Surface-to-air missiles, two superimposed Standard ER launchers forward, one Talos twin launcher aft; AS weapons, one ASROC 8-tube launcher immediately behind the bridge amidships; guns, two single 5in 38-cal one each side amidships; torpedo tubes, two triple Mk 32 12·7in (324mm) mounts one each side of the superstructure just forward of the bridge.
Propulsion: Two Westinghouse CIW reactors, two sets GE steam turbines. Approx 40,000shp each, maximum speed over 30kts.

Long Beach (CGN-9, ex CGN-160, ex CLGN-160) was the first surface warship to have nuclear propulsion, and was also the first to be armed entirely with guided missiles. She was originally intended to be a 7,800 ton standard displacement guided missile frigate with a single Terrier SAM launcher. Before the design was finalized in 1956 the size had almost doubled and the armament considerably increased. She was completed with two Terrier SAM twin launchers superfiring forward and a Talos launcher aft. She was originally designed to carry Regulus II SSMs. This was a nuclear armed strategic cruise missile with a range of about 1,000 miles at ▶

Right: *Long Beach* in port. Because of her nuclear propulsion she has not always been welcomed in foreign ports, especially as she was the first ever surface ship with such power.

Below: *Long Beach* at sea in 1976. The huge 'billboards' around the bridge are fixed antennas for the SPS-32 radar (horizontal) and the SPS-33 radar (vertical). The antennas are fixed, but by means of electronic scanning 360° coverage is obtained.

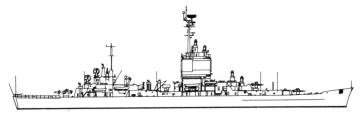

Above: USS *Long Beach* (CGN-9) was commissioned on 9 Sep 1961.

Above: *Long Beach* at sea. In 1964 a USN all-nuclear task force sailed round the world without needing to replenish in 65 days.

Right: This bow view of the *Long Beach* shows the huge bridge structure resulting from the SPS-32 and -33 antennas.

a speed of Mach 2. When this was cancelled in favor of Polaris ICBMs, it was planned to fit eight of these in tubes amidships. However, Polaris has only been fitted in submarines and *Long Beach* was finally completed without any SSMs or ICBMs. Instead, she mounts an ASROC launcher amidships. Laid down in 1957, she was completed in 1961 at a cost of nearly $333 million. The forward superstructure is similar to that fitted to the nuclear aircraft carrier *Enterprise* (CVN-65). It is a large square structure with fixed "Billboard" antennae for the SPS-32 surface search and target designation and SPS-33 height finding radars. The aft superstructure is much smaller, and since the 1962–63 refit it has been flanked by two 5in guns, which were fitted to counter the threat from low-flying aircraft and fast patrol boats, neither of which could be dealt with by missiles. *Long Beach* was completed as an escort for nuclear aircraft carriers, and is intended to deal with air and sub-surface threats. At present she relies mainly on carrier-borne aircraft for defense against surface attack, though her present missiles have a limited surface-to-surface capability. In company with *Enterprise* (CVN-65) and *Bainbridge* (CGN-25), *Long Beach* showed the advantages of an all nuclear task force during Operation Sea Orbit in 1964, when these three nuclear powered ships sailed round the world in 65 days without needing to replenish. *Long Beach* underwent her first major refit and refuelling in 1966–67, after steaming over 160,000 miles on her first reactor cores, much of it at sustained high speed. Her radars were updated in 1970, and she will shortly be undergoing her "mid-life" refit. She will probably be refitted with the Aegis system at a cost of over $400 million, which will eliminate some of the shortcomings in her surface-to-surface and close range weapons and update her electronics.

Los Angeles Class

Nuclear-powered attack submarines
Eleven in service, twenty more ordered.

Country of origin: United States
Displacement: 6,900 tons submerged.
Dimensions: Length overall 358ft 10in (109·7m); beam 32ft 11in (10·1m); draught 31ft 11in (9·8m).
Armament: Torpedo tubes, four 21in (533mm) amidships.
Propulsion: One D2G reactor, two sets steam turbines. Total approx 30,000shp on one shaft, submerged speed approx 35kts.

The first *Los Angeles* class Nuclear Attack Submarine (SSN) entered service in 1976, and a total of twenty-three are on order at present. These follow the experimental *Glenard P Lipscomb* (SSN-685), built between 1971–74 and are much larger than previous SSNs. They have a much higher submerged speed, and the increase in displacement is necessary to allow this and to enable them to carry all the electronics and weapons systems that are fitted. They have the BQQ-5 sonar system, and can operate Subroc, Sub-Harpoon and submarine launched cruise missiles as well as conventional and wire-guided torpedoes. Thus, like all the later US SSNs, although they are basically intended to hunt other submarines and to protect the SSBNs, they can also be used without modification to sink ships at long range with Sub-Harpoon, and when they enter service they can use the new cruise missiles to fire nuclear warheads at targets well inland. It is possible that with the new US emphasis on strategic cruise missiles, this role may be increased, and the new cruise missiles will in any case be used to attack surface targets at ten times the range of the existing 70 miles range Sub-Harpoon in a tactical rile. Considerable delays in the shipbuilding programme for the class meant that almost five years elapsed between keel-laying and commissioning of the lead ship.

Above: *Los Angeles* class. Note the great length of the hull.

Above: The launching of USS *Philadelphia* (SSN 690) on 19 October 1974 at the Electric Boat Company yard. The flag not only adds to the colour of the occasion but also protects the highly classified bow sonar from inquisitive eyes. Eleven of these boats are currently in service, a further ten are under construction and another eleven have been ordered; delivery is at a rate of about one per year until the mid-1980s, when building will be speeded-up.

Left: USS *Los Angeles* (SSN-688) at speed on the surface, which is not her natural habitat, her design being optimised for underwater operation. The aim of the USN is to achieve an attack submarine force level of 90 boats by the mid-1980s.

Below: Another view of USS *Los Angeles* running on the surface. Special efforts have been made in this design to achieve really quiet underwater performance, and although details are naturally classified, it is reported that this has been achieved. A version of the Harpoon missile has been developed which can be launched from a torpedo tube and fired underwater against ships.

Nimitz Class

Aircraft carriers

Two ships (plus one building): *Nimitz* (CVN-68), *Eisenhower* (CVN-69).

Country of origin: United States
Displacement: 81,600 tons (91,400 full load).
Dimensions: Length overall 1,090ft 3in (332·9m); deck width overall 251ft 6in (76·8m); beam 133ft 9in (40·8m); draught 42ft 6in (13m).
Aircraft: Over 90 aircraft and helicopters.
Armament: Surface-to-air missiles, three BPDMS Sea Sparrow 8-tube launchers on sponsons one to starboard forward and one each side aft.
Propulsion: Two A4W reactors, four sets GE steam turbines. Total approx 280,000shp on four shafts, maximum speed approx 33kts.

It was decided in October 1963 that *John F Kennedy* (CV-67) should be conventionally powered because of the massive expense of nuclear powered carriers, and in February 1965 Secretary of Defense McNamara announced in Congress that the attack carrier force was to be reduced by two ships to 13 because of growing doubts about their utility and vulnerability, especially in view of their immense cost. However, the effectiveness of the carrier operations off Vietnam brought a change of heart, and in February 1966 McNamara told Congress that he had reassessed the need and was planning to ask for 15 attack carriers again. *Enterprise* (CVN-65) had demonstrated how valuable the extra freedom of action allowed by using nuclear power could be, and four nuclear powered aircraft carriers were included in McNamara's new total. On 1 July 1966 funds were provided for *Nimitz* (CVN-68), and she was then due for completion in 1971 with her sisters CVN-69 and CVN-70 due in 1973 and 1975. The facts of the future were to be very different. Only one American shipyard, the Newport News Shipbuilding and Dry Dock Co. which built *Enterprise* (CVN-65), was able to build them. *Nimitz* (CVN-68) was laid down in 1968, but problems beset her construction at all points. Though she required only two reactors as opposed to eight in *Enterprise* (CVN-65), delays in delivering and testing the components of the new A4W/A1G reactors caused slippage which was exacerbated by shortages of labor. As a result *Nimitz* (CVN-68) was not commissioned in 1971 but on 3 May

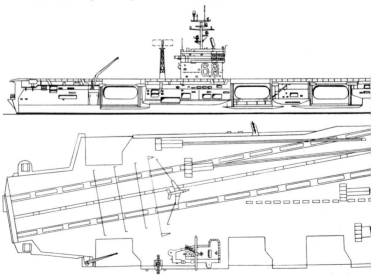

1975; her next sister, *Dwight D Eisenhower* (CVN-69), in 1977 instead of 1973; and *Carl Vinson* (CVN-70) was not laid down until October 1975 with a tentative delivery date in 1981 instead of 1975. As a result, costs have shot up, and while the price of *Nimitz* (CVN-68) was $1·881 billion, the next pair will be over $2 billion each.

These three ships are slightly larger than *Enterprise* (CVN-65), but their machinery is smaller, advantage having been taken of improvements in reactor design to reduce their number from eight to two with only a slight reduction in power and speed. This enables them to carry a fifth again as much aviation fuel as the earlier nuclear carrier, and they can also carry more ammunition and stores, thus further reducing their dependence on external supply. They also have a greater complement, more aircraft, and a different radar (SPS 48 in place of SPS 32/33). Planning for a fourth ship ▶

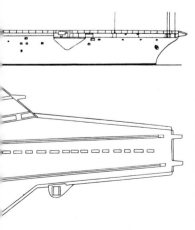

Above: There are 48 aircraft parked on the flight-deck of USS *Nimitz* in this picture, which is about half her normal complement. The arrival of a Task Force (including one of these carriers and her embarked air wing) can completely alter the balance of power in a threatened area of the world. Nevertheless there is more to military power than just hardware; the political will to use it is also necessary.

Left: USS *Nimitz* (CVN-68). These mighty ships displace 91,487 tons at full load and can accommodate over 90 aircraft. Their war complement, including aviation staff, is a massive 6,300. Their nuclear reactors have sufficient energy for some 13 years of operations.

was temporarily in abeyance as a result of continuing doubts over these ships' utility and cost effectiveness. However, although it appeared almost certain in 1975-76 that the nuclear aircraft carrier would be abandoned in favor of a spartan, conventionally powered *Essex* sized ship, the proponents of the nuclear powered carrier again appeared to be coming to the fore in 1977, and preliminary funding provided for a fourth *Nimitz* class aircraft carrier, but this was vetoed by President Carter in 1978.

Right: The *Nimitz* in the Mediterranean in company with the nuclear-powered cruiser USS *South Carolina* (CGN-37). Such a Task Force can deploy quickly to any part of the oceans and remain almost indefinitely. The limiting factor would be aviation fuel for the *Nimitz's* aircraft.

Below: The *Nimitz* is replenished at sea. This class probably represents the ultimate in carrier development for fixed-wing conventional take-off aircraft, and the British and Soviet change to V/STOL aircraft and smaller carriers shows the future.

Ohio Class

Nuclear-powered ballistic missile submarines
Three building, four more ordered.

Country of origin: United States
Displacement: 16,000 surface (18,700 submerged).
Dimensions: Length overall 560ft (170·7m); beam 42ft (12·8m); draught 35ft 6in (10·8m).
Armament: Submarine launched ballistic missiles, twenty-four vertical tubes for Trident 1 in two rows of twelve in hull behind fin; torpedo tubes, four 21in (533mm) in bow.
Propulsion: One GE S8G reactor, one set GE steam turbines. Total shp on one shaft, and submerged speed not known.

While the program of upgrading the later Polaris SLBM submarines to carry the Poseidon SLBM was underway in the early 1970s, a new SLBM program was under development. This was to provide a much longer range missile, the Trident 1 SLBM with a range of 4,000 miles, and a huge 18,700 ton submarine to carry 24 of them. In due course, probably in the early 1980s, it was intended to introduce the improved Trident II SLBM with a 6,000 mile range to be retrofitted in place of the earlier missile. While Congress baulked at the immense cost of this new system, the Soviet Navy introduced their own long range SLBM, the 4,200 mile range SSN-8, in the *Delta* class SSBN in 1972. In 1976 the first increased range SSN-8s (6,450 miles) were fired. The US reaction was to speed up development of the Trident programme, and the first *Ohio* class Nuclear Ballistic Missile Submarine (SSBN) *Ohio* (SSBN-726) was laid down on 10 April 1976. *Michigan* (SSBN-727) has also been laid down, and a further eight are on order. They were due to enter service from 1979 but have slipped three years. The eventual number of Trident SLBM-carrying submarines depends on two main factors. The first is the result of the SALT

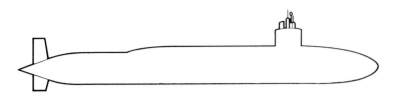

Above: The *Ohio* class will be the largest submarines ever built.

(Strategic Arms Limitation Talks) agreement currently being negotiated between America and Russia, and any subsequent agreements. These will once again determine the maximum number of SLBMs that each side will tolerate the other having. The other factor is the development of the new types of long range cruise missiles, some of which can be used in a strategic role when launched from an ordinary 21in (533mm) submarine torpedo tube. Further developments in this field may restrict the need for a large number of SLBMs. However, the great advantage of the current generation of extremely long range SLBMs is that they can be launched from America's and Russia's home waters, thus making it extremely difficult to destroy the missiles before they have been fired. This makes the immense size of the *Ohio*s less significant, because although they are an immense target they are unlikely to be exposed to serious attack.

Below: An artist's impression of one of the mighty *Ohio* class submarines at sea. Clearly visible is the long casing over the launch tubes for the 24 Trident 1 missiles, which have a range of some 4,000 nautical miles and carry a large number (14+) independently targeted re-entry vehicles (MIRV) with a very high degree of accuracy. *Ohio* class submarines will be the largest underwater vehicles ever, with a submerged displacement of 18,700 tons, which is double that of the Soviet *Delta 1* (q.v.).

Pegasus Class

Patrol hydrofoils
One ship (plus four ordered): *Pegasus* (PHN-1).

Country of origin: United States
Displacement: 190 tons (221 full load).
Dimensions: foilborne; length overall 131ft 2in (40m); beam 28ft 2in (8·6m); draught 7ft 6in (2·3m).
Armament: Surface-to-surface missiles, eight Harpoon aft; guns, one single 3in 62-cal forward.
Propulsion: Foilborne; one GE gas turbine. Total 18,000shp, maximum speed over 48kts. Hullborne; two MTU diesels. Total 1,600bhp, maximum speed 12kts.

The *Pegasus* class Missile armed Patrol Hydrofoil (PHM) was developed by Boeing from several earlier civil and military craft, including the USS *Tucumcari* (PGH-2) which was built between 1966–68. They are all submerged foil hydrofoils, and they differ in having one hydrofoil at the bows and two (one each side) aft, whereas other hydrofoils have two foils forward and one aft. The Boeing system, combined with a computer, gives quicker reactions and a smoother ride in rough water. *Pegasus* (PHM-1) was originally intended to be the prototype for a number of hydrofoils with the same hull and machinery but with differing armaments for the United States, Italy and Germany. The German boats were to have been equipped with Exocet SSMs. However, by the time *Pegasus* (PHM-1) was built in 1973–6, all three countries had had second thoughts. Although the PHM offers a heavy armanent on a small, very fast and highly manouvrable hull, it is also extremely expensive, and it was considered that cheaper and less sophisticated vessels might be better for the short range tasks that *Pegasus* was designed to perform. However, the project seems to have been revived by Congress, who have given the go-ahead for PHM 3–6. In addition to the PHMs, the USN has an interest in several other unconventional types of ship. This includes the SWATH (Small Waterplane Twin Hull) research ship *Kaimalino*, and the Hovercraft or SES (Surface Effect Ships). A number of British and American SES have been tested, including the 100 ton Bell SES-100B, and so impressed has the USN been by the potential of these vessels for ASW and Minesweeping that they have gone ahead with the design of a 3,000 ton LSES. This will be optimized for AS warfare and carry two helicopters or a V/STOL aircraft.

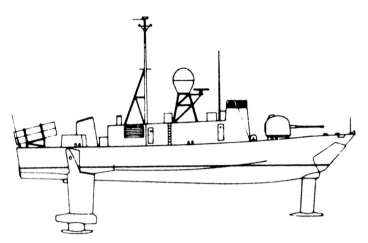

Above: *Pegasus* was designed as a NATO standard hydrofoil.

Above: USS *Pegasus* (PCM(H)-1) hull-borne on patrol with an *Asheville* class patrol gunboat. Armed with eight Harpoon SSMs and one 76mm gun, these craft are capable of 48 knots foil-borne and 12 knots hullborne. Six are to be built by 1983.

Left: USS *Pegasus* at speed on her foils. As with so many plans for NATO standardisation, this one, too, came to nought; the Italians are proceeding with their own Sparviero design (q.v.) and the other countries have lost interest. The USN will procure six of these craft at a total cost of $272.7 million.

Spruance Class

Destroyers

31 ships including *Spruance* (DD-963), *Caron* (DD-970)

Country of origin: United States
Displacement: 7,300 tons full load.
Dimensions: Length overall 563ft 4in (171·1m); beam 55ft (17·6m); draught 29ft (8·8m).
Aircraft: Two Kaman SH-2F Seasprite or one Sikorsky SH-3D Sea King with hangar and pad at aft end of superstructure.
Armament: Surface-to-air missiles, one BPDMS Sea Sparrow 8-tube launcher to be fitted on break of quarterdeck aft; guns, two single 5in 54-cal Mk 45 one forward and one right aft; AS weapons, one ASROC 8-tube launcher in front of bridge; torpedo tubes, six Mk 32 12·7in (324mm) tubes three each side at stern.
Propulsion: Four sets GE gas turbines. Total 80,000shp on two shafts, maximum speed over 30kts.

Whilst the US built up a considerable force of carrier-escort guided missile destroyers in the years after World War II, she relied on the ageing wartime destroyers to provide the bulk of her general purpose escorts. Although many of the *Fletcher, Allen M Sumner* and *Gearing* class destroyers were modernized in the early 1960s, no new hulls were built, and by the late 1960s they were worn out and well overdue for replacement. Although some still remain in reserve, most have been transferred to other navies or scrapped. The *Spruance* class were designed to replace them. They are the first large American warships to be powered totally by gas turbines, and are intended primarily for AS work. Because the weapons systems and crew cost more than the ship herself, the *Spruances* are large and extremely seaworthy ships with a relatively small number of weapons, so that a large number could be built with the available money. This policy has excited a great deal of criticism, not least amongst officers in the USN, and their lack of armament has been widely deplored. However, sheer numbers of ships were necessary in a hurry to replace the enormous quantity of World War II vessels, and the large size of the ships, combined with the rectangular shape of the superstructure, means that new weapons can easily be installed, and new electronics modules added to the ones already there. The only problem

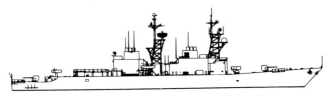

Above: *Spruance* class is large and roomy but lightly armed.

is the cost. In keeping with the desire to keep the ships as simple and cheap as possible, the funnels are arranged directly over the engines, so they are staggered on different sides of the hull. In an attempt to reduce costs still further, the entire class is being built by one firm on one specially constructed production line. Unfortunately, this Total Ship Procurement Package, so far from reducing costs, has itself caused many problems and expenses. Thirty *Spruance*s were authorized. The first was delivered in 1976, four years after it was begun and they are still under construction. They will be retrofitted with Harpoon as soon as it becomes available. Perhaps the most successful aspect of these ships is the very small number of crew. It is possible that the basic hull design may be used for a new anti-aircraft escort. A version fitted with the new Mk 26 combined SAM/ASM/SSM launcher and Aegis, the DDG-47, has been designed to replace the *Charles F Adams* class DDGs, but it has not been authorized as yet by Congress. **continued ▶**

Above: USS *Spruance* (DD-963) at sea. The primary mission of these ships is anti-submarine warfare including operations as an integral part of attack carrier task forces.

Left: USS *Spruance* on her shakedown cruise in the Atlantic in 1975. The 'Total Ship Procurement Package', intended to reduce time and expense, led to confusion, cost over-runs and lost time, and the whole programme is running late and is criticised by Congress.

USS *Kinkaid* (DD-965) of the *Spruance* class. The aim was to keep the design as simple and as cheap as possible so, for example, the funnels are directly over the engines and not, as is more usual, on the centreline, as is shown clearly in this picture. The cost-cutting exercise has not been a success.

Tarawa Class

Amphibious assault ships
Five ships including *Tarawa* (LHA-1), *Nassau* (LHA-4).

Country of origin: United States
Displacement: 39,300 tons full load.
Dimensions: Length overall 820ft (237·8m); beam 106ft (32·3m); draught 27ft 6in (8·4m).
Aircraft: Typically 30 Boeing Vertol UH-46 Sea Knight and Sikorsky CH-53 Sea Stallion helicopters.
Armament: Surface-to-air missiles, two BPDMS Sea Sparrow 8-tube launchers one just forward of the island and one on the port quarter; guns, three single 5in 54-cal one each side of the bow and one on the starboard quarter.
Propulsion: Two sets Westinghouse steam turbines. Total 70,000shp on two shafts, maximum speed 24kts.

The *Tarawa* class Amphibious Assault Ships (LHA) are designed to fulfil the functions of both the LPHs and the LPDs, by being able to carry a battalion group of about 1,800 Marines and land them and their equipment by both helicopters and landing craft. Although this means that the loss of one ship would be more damaging than before, it saves the cost of a large and complex vessel and its crew. They have a full length continuous flight deck, with a large rectangular island to starboard. The helicopter hangar is in the aft part of the ship, and it is connected to the flight deck by a portside elevator and another at the stern on the centerline. The forward part of the hull at hangar deck level is used for stores and equipment, which, as in the *Iwo Jimas,* is brought up to the flight deck by two small elevators. Beneath the hangar aft there is a dock large enough to contain four *1610* class LCUs. Side thrusters are fitted to make docking and undocking easier. Nine of these ships were ordered under a Total Package Procurement Contract from Litton Industries, but as in the case of the *Spruances* this has proved a failure. Cost overruns have been considerable and completion of the class was delayed by between two to four years whilst the problems were resolved. Four *Tarawas* have been cancelled, and although the first was laid down in 1971, by 1980 only four were in service.

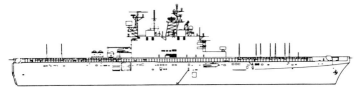

Above: USS *Tarawa* (LHA-1), commissioned 29 May 1976.

Above: *Tarawa* was launched on 1 December 1973. The design is a mixture of an aircraft carrier and a Landing Platform Dock (LPD) and makes an interesting comparison with the *Ivan Rogov* (q.v.).

Below: USS *Tarawa* at sea. The flight-deck can operate a maximum of nine CH-53 Sea Stallion or twelve CH-46 Sea Knight helicopters. AV-8A Harrier V/STOL aircraft can also be operated. Personnel accommodation is available for some 1,800 men, and trucks and landing craft are also carried. This major concentration of resources in one hull makes a very attractive target.

Look out for these other
SUPER-VALUE GUIDES!

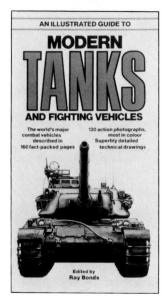

* Each has 160 fact-filled pages

* Each is colorfully illustrated with action photographs and technical drawings

* Each contains concisely presented data and accurate descriptions of major international weapons

* Each represents terrific value

Following soon:
Illustrated guides to

**German, Italian and Japanese
FIGHTERS AND ATTACK AIRCRAFT
of World War II**

**BOMBERS
of World War II**

detailing the exciting combat aircraft that fought in the most ferocious war in history

.... thousands of facts and figures
.... hundreds of action photos, many in color
.... superb color profiles depicting unit markings
.... highly detailed three-view line drawings

Your military library will be incomplete without them.

PRINTED IN BELGIUM BY

INTERNATIONAL BOOK PRODUCTION